Honesty's Travesty

ARTHUR O.R. THORMANN

Honesty's Travesty

ISBN 978-1-7770735-2-7

Publisher: Specfab Industries Ltd.
                    13559 - 123A Avenue
                    Edmonton, Alberta, Canada
                    T5L 2Z1
                    Telephone: 780-454-6396

Publication assistance by

PAGEMASTER
PUBLISHING
PageMaster.ca

The author is grateful to Robert Lynn, Pamela Sigvaldason, Garett Llorente, and FriesenPress for their valuable advice, and to Shutterstock for the book cover image of the businessman on a tightrope.

The search for truth, if successful,
may be liberating for some,
but it will seldom result
in universal happiness.

1

When the phone rang it startled Jack Malone. He was always annoyed at disruptions when he was engrossed in a set of specifications.

"Hello?"

"Jack, this is Harry Broughton. I hope I'm not disrupting anything."

Harry Broughton was the President and CEO of MDF Industrial Constructors Inc., a company that contracts for erection of industrial projects such as heavy oil upgraders, refineries, pumping stations, and power generation, water treatment and production and processing plants. Harry occupied a large executive suite at MDF's head office in Toronto.

"You are, Harry, but that's okay. What's on your mind?"

"When are you planning to return to Toronto, Jack?"

"Early next week, probably Tuesday. I want to meet with our Contracts Committee to discuss some penalty provisions the owners insist on for the New Brunswick Refinery."

Harry had sent Jack to MDF's Maritime Division in New Brunswick to discuss complications that MDF might encounter building the refinery with division manager Jim Rowe, and to prepare a risk analysis for the project.

Jack ran his own division near Toronto; one of his special talents included identifying construction risks, a skill that was lacking in most of MDF's division managers. "I'm heading out of town on Tuesday. Can you make it Monday morning, Jack, say eleven?"

"It'll be tight for me, but yes, I think I can make it Monday. What should I prepare myself for?"

"Nothing specific, Jack, but bring along your Claims and Issues Report—the one you had prepared for our last management meeting."

"Okay, Harry."

"I'll set up a Contracts Committee meeting for ten o'clock on Monday. After the meeting, come and see me. I'll treat you to a special lunch. Have a good weekend."

Before Jack returned to his specifications he called Betty, Jim Rowe's secretary, on the intercom.

"Betty, please make arrangements for me to take a flight out to Toronto on Sunday afternoon, and make me a hotel reservation at The Fairmont Royal York Hotel downtown."

"Will do. For how many nights?"

"Two. I'm sure I won't finish all my business in Toronto on Monday."

"Okay. Is there anything you need typed up?"

"Thanks, Betty. I'll let you know later today.

Jack liked Betty. She was very thorough, very dependable, and good-looking to boot.

Jack arrived at the Fairmont in Toronto just after nine o'clock on Sunday evening. He checked in, settled in, and called room service, ordering a glass of milk, toast, and scrambled eggs. He knew that a light supper always assured him a better sleep.

After breakfast on Monday he took a taxi to MDF's head office. The meeting with the Contracts Committee lasted just over an hour. As usual, the committee members kept stretching things out with a number of redundant questions, which Jack tried to answer patiently.

Fiona, Harry's private secretary, a tall brunette in her late thirties, greeted him with a warm smile.

"Go right in, Jack, he's expecting you."

Harry was sitting behind a huge mahogany desk with nothing on it except the business section of *The Globe and Mail*. He got up, came around the desk, shook Jack's hand, and led him to some leather armchairs in front of a glass coffee table in a corner of his office, by the window.

Harry was in his early fifties, and Jack in his mid-forties. Both men had six-foot, athletic figures. Harry had graying blond hair, set off by a ruddy, sun-tanned complexion. He wore a beige suit, a light-brown, open-necked checkered shirt, and suede shoes. Jack had brown hair and light complexion; he wore a dark brown suit, white shirt with maroon tie, and black leather shoes. It was obvious that both men liked to dress well.

They made themselves comfortable and Harry asked, "How did your meeting go?"

"Okay, I guess. The committee members were not overly concerned with the strict penalty provisions."

"I take it you are concerned with the penalty provisions?"

"I'm always concerned with penalty provisions—especially with allowing for them in the tender." In the construction industry a tender is an offer to perform construction work for payment by the owner.

"Hmm. Anything I can do?" Harry asked.

"I don't think so, Harry. I'll insert some options in my risk analysis."

"Good! Let's go and have some lunch."

Harry had decided on his yacht club for lunch. He said he liked the fish menu it offered. In addition, this gave him an opportunity to check on and show off his pride and joy—his oversized yacht.

They ordered poached pickerel, one of the club's specialties, and a bottle of French Chenin Blanc to go with the fish. During the meal Harry related a few of his yachting stories to Jack.

"Do you limit your yachting to Lake Ontario, Harry?"

"Not at all. We sail right down the St. Lawrence River into the Gulf of St. Lawrence—occasionally as far as Cape Breton."

"Must be fun!"

"It's more than that, Jack—it's outright adventurous! In fact, we're planning to head south next summer, down to the Bahamas."

"Isn't that a bit dangerous?"

"No, we won't be sailing too far from shore."

"Do you need another deckhand?"

Harry laughed. "Let's order coffees and brandy."

After the waiter left Harry continued. "The reason I wanted to meet with you, Jack, is the problems we are having with construction claims."

Jack gave Harry a questioning look. MDF's contracts usually consisted of a fixed price. Monetary claims, in addition to the fixed price, only arise when things go wrong—unexpected construction delays or work disruptions that affect production.

"The problems are manifold," said Harry. "The worst part is the damage to our customer relations."

He looked at Jack to make sure he followed. Jack nodded. "Then there is our own damage," Harry continued. "We never recover what we have lost."

Jack nodded again, even more emphatically.

"Our reputation is at stake," Harry went on. "Mainly because our customers feel we're gouging them—and I appreciate why they feel that way."

He sat in silence for a while, sipping his brandy.

"But if they're not paying us what we're asking in our claims, what makes them think they're being gouged?" Jack wanted to know.

"Because in most cases they feel we're trying to make up for our own deficiencies, and they shouldn't be paying us any claims at all."

He took another sip from his snifter. "Besides," he continued, "our division managers have become too reliant on construction claims—mostly to cover the shortcomings of their construction tenders—and that is what hurts our reputation the most. Our customers wouldn't mind so much paying for legitimate claims, but they resent being taken advantage of."

They were both silent again.

"I presume you include me in your assessment of our division managers. Is this why you called me in for a meeting, Harry?" Jack asked.

"No, no, Jack. I'm sorry if I gave you the wrong impression. No—in fact, I've taken a close look at your claims record, and I must commend you on your honesty. That's probably why your claims payment ratio is higher than that of the other division managers. I was also impressed with your Claims and Issues Report at our last management meeting. You gave a good claims process outline that treats both parties fairly, and you pointed out some fallacies of claims."

Jack nodded again and both men were lost in their thoughts for a while.

"No," said Harry, "I want you to take on the job of investigating the validity of our claims before we submit them to our customers."

Jack looked startled. "You want me to rat on my fellow division managers?"

"They won't be your fellow division managers if you take on the job, Jack. Your division will be managed by your second-in-command, and your new title will be VP of Customer Relations."

"Our division managers will still consider me one of theirs," Jack objected.

"Not if you play it smart, Jack. Besides, would they be any happier if I hired an outside consultant to do the job? I think they probably trust your judgment and sincerity more than that of any outsider."

"To whom would I report?"

"You would report to me directly."

"And what autonomy would I have?"

"You would have full autonomy, Jack, but, when you feel you're too far out on a limb, you would come to me for consultation. In that regard, I have complete confidence in you."

"What would be my job parameters?"

"You will travel to various company divisions and/or company projects and make a thorough analysis of potential claims. You will then report to me on the validity and financial feasibility of these potential claims. I will decide whether to proceed with or to abandon them. If the decision is to proceed with a claim, you will also help finalize it and assist in negotiations for its settlement."

Harry gave him a sincere look. "In other words, Jack—investigate, authenticate, and negotiate, but do not prevaricate!"

He signaled the waiter to bring them another round.

"My experience has been that the direct approach is the most successful one, and honesty is the best policy. Too many of our managers are trying to get away with something, and our company, as well as our customer relationships, suffer because of this approach."

Jack nodded in complete agreement.

"One more thing," Harry added. "I may also ask you to give short seminars at our managers' meetings regarding the folly of relying too much on claims."

Jack nodded again. "Do you have a specific claim in mind at the moment?" Jack wanted to know.

"Yes, I do. Brian's claim against the Northern Alberta Oil Upgrader Consortium—he calls it 'the Consortium.'"

Brian Forbes was the Alberta Division Manager. The Consortium was formed by a group of oil companies, and the upgrader converted heavy oil into lighter oil. It was a fast-track project for which the Consortium had required eight construction phase tenders. MDF had been the successful bidder on four phases. Three of the four phases were finished and settled. The unsettled phase was one of the heavy piping phases. It could have been an eighty million dollar contract, but the Consortium supplied most of the heavy materials, which left MDF with an intense labor contract of about twenty million dollars. Rumor had it that MDF's bid for this phase was substantially low.

"How will Brian react to my investigations, which he will no doubt perceive as meddling—and I wouldn't blame him?"

"If you agree to take the job, I will immediately send a letter to all our division managers outlining our aims and your authority with respect to dealing with their claims."

"How long do I have to decide?"

"Time is of the essence, Jack. Why are you still hesitating? You can also expect a decent increase in your salary, I might add."

"It'll be a big change to the work I'm used to doing and to my present lifestyle, Harry."

"As far as the work you're used to doing is concerned, the new job will only give you additional challenges, if I read you right. Regarding your lifestyle, since you're single now, you may even enhance it by the required amount of travel. Am I not right?"

Jack gave Harry a sharp look. He had recently ended a brief relationship with a wonderful but demanding woman. To what extent did Harry keep track of his employees' private lives?

"Okay, you have me convinced. When do I start?"

"Go back to your division and rearrange things there. Then report back to me next Monday and we'll discuss a few more details before you leave for Calgary. I'll have an office ready for you on my floor, and for the time being feel free to ask Fiona for any secretarial help you may need."

"Thanks, Harry. And thanks also for the excellent lunch."

2

Jack liked his new office. It was small compared to Harry's suite, but well appointed and with a good view of Toronto's skyline, which he inspected vaguely.

The phone gave off a subdued buzz and he picked up the receiver: "Jack Malone."

"Hello Jack. Brian Forbes. I hear congratulations are in order on your new appointment. When are you heading out to see us in Calgary?"

"Thanks, Brian. Next week sometime, I hope."

"Anything you need from me before you head out?"

"I'm glad you asked. In fact, I was going to call you this morning to send me an electronic copy of your estimate for the Consortium's crude oil upgrader, including the estimates for all approved extra work."

"That'll be a huge file, Jack. We may have trouble transmitting it. There are over two hundred estimates for the extra work the engineers have approved to date."

"Well give it a try. Our service provider allows us to send pretty large files."

"Okay, Jack. Let me know when you're coming. I'll pick you up from the airport."

"Will do. Take care of yourself!"

Jack disconnected the line. then dialed Bill Snider's number. Bill Snider was a friend of his working in the accounting department.

"Bill, Jack here. Does head office still track all purchases for large projects?"

"Sure thing, Jack."

"Would it be possible for you to create an Excel spreadsheet comparing estimate items with purchased items?"

"Theoretically, yes, Jack. But I would have to add a column with a code for each different item."

"Is that fairly easy to do?"

"Adding the column is easy, but adding the codes takes time. We would also have to create a master list of all the codes for easy reference."

"How long would all that take?"

"Depends on the number of different items. If I use an electronic replication method, it wouldn't take all that long. If I had time enough to do it, about a day for two or three hundred items."

"We wouldn't have many more items than that if we excluded the nuts and bolts."

"When do you need to have this job completed, Jack?"

"I would like to see it completed by the end of next week, Bill, which means you'd probably have to start on it ASAP. Is that possible?"

"It's possible, but I would have to push off some other work and clear it with the CFO."

"That shouldn't be a problem. He's been briefed by Harry as to my special assignments, which will take priority unless overruled by Harry."

"Do you have the estimate in electronic format?"

"I will have it later today."

"Well, let me know when you're ready to go, Jack."

Jack hung up and walked to Fiona's office.

"Are you free for lunch today, Fiona?"

"Where do you have in mind?"

"How about the Mövenpick?"

She rolled her eyes: "Okay."

"What's your preference?"

"The Globe Bistro."

"Fine with me."

After they had placed their orders, Fiona asked, "Is this a social gesture of yours, or do you want to discuss business, Jack?"

"I just want to get to know you better, Fiona. Harry mentioned that I should go to you for any secretarial help I may need."

"I may arrange that for you, but I wouldn't necessarily do it myself. Harry is a pretty demanding boss, you know."

"I didn't know that. I thought he spent most of his time yachting."

"He does, but he conducts a lot of business from his yacht and I'm his right arm on land."

"How long have you worked for him?"

"Six years now."

"And the job is satisfying, I presume?"

"Very. I've never had such an interesting job before. Never a dull day in this business."

"I'd have to agree with you, especially with my new mandate."

"Do you look forward to that?"

"With mixed feelings, Fiona. All our division managers are personal friends of mine and ratting on them gives me the creeping willies."

"Why would you be ratting on them? Wouldn't you just investigate the feasibility of their claims and advise Harry in this regard?"

"Yes, but if a claim isn't feasible, I would also have to report to Harry why it isn't, and that may involve divulging a manager's shortcomings, which could even lead to firings!"

"I see what you mean. Then let me ask you this—why did you undertake the task of doing it if it bothers you so much, Jack?"

"I don't know, Fiona. I've got rocks in my head, I suppose. Harry can be very persuasive, as you know."

"Anything I can do to help?"

"Thanks. You've done it already. I needed to talk to someone sympathetic about my feelings."

Back at the office, Jack opened his email inbox and found Brian's transmission of the upgrader estimates. Brian was right—it was a big file. He looked at it briefly and then forwarded it to Bill Snider. He hoped that the estimates and the purchases record would be a close match, for Brian's sake.

Next, he started reading the general conditions section of the upgrader's specifications and decided to retire to his new condominium to finish reading it in more comfort.

The general conditions for this contract had as many weasel or escape clauses in them as general conditions of other projects he had seen, mostly to protect the owners and engineers of the project. As usual, forget about fairness—the contractor had to fend for himself, if he was smart enough to know how.

What bothered him the most was the general provision that disallowed construction delays because of extra work. This meant that every one of the estimates for extra work had to specify and request a schedule extension, if required, and the engineers might deny it. Furthermore, the extra estimates should identify any production impact anticipated on the original contract work. If the contractor failed to justify this adequately he was up the creek, as it were.

Jack got up to stretch and pour himself a glass of sherry. He could already imagine the various problems he may encounter in this regard and made himself a special mental note to examine all extra estimates and tender submissions very carefully for potential flaws.

Jack decided to stay home for the evening. He turned on the TV and switched to BBC's World-News channel. There never seemed to be much good news anymore—suicide-bombings in Iraq and Afghanistan again, the American president's problem with unemployment, several European countries on the verge of bankruptcy with economies collapsing everywhere, scientists' concern with global warming and climate change. Disgusted, he turned the TV off and made himself a ham and cheese omelet for supper. After he cleaned up the dishes he chose a mystery movie to watch for the evening.

The next morning Jack gave Brian a call. "Brian, could you also email me the extra construction work tenders for the upgrader?"

"I could, but whatever for, Jack?"

"I want to check on our conditions regarding schedule extensions and impacts to the work of the original contract work."

"I'll send you the tenders, but you might as well know that we encountered a problem in that regard."

"What kind of a problem?"

"The engineers refused to accept our extension requests as well as our estimates for the impact on our contracted work. They literally eliminated these conditions prior to approving the extra work."

"How did you react to that?"

"We countered with letters reserving the right to submit a claim for these items at a later date."

"Well, send me all correspondence relating to the extra work, Brian."

"Okay."

Jack, too, had run into projects where the engineers had disallowed schedule extensions and impact claims as part of the extra work estimate. Their argument was usually that the owners' production will suffer because of a schedule extension, and that a contractor can only establish impacts properly after all of his construction work is completed. The problem that a contractor may have with this argument is collecting for the unapproved outlays he has expended. As lawyers will tell us, possession is nine-tenths of the law.

Jack called Fiona. "Is Harry free this morning, Fiona?"

"Harry is never free. What do you have in mind?"

"I'd like to have a few minutes of his time to discuss an issue that came up this morning."

"I'll get back to you."

She phoned him back a few minutes later, "Harry will see you at eleven."

"Thanks, Fiona."

"Don't mention it."

Jack swiveled his chair around and glanced out of the window for a few moments. The upgrader claim problem had just taken on a new dimension. He hoped Brian had employed the only method to deal with this situation, namely keeping track of time and labor for every extra, which separated the original contract work for easier assessment later.

He decided to check on Bill's project before seeing Harry.

"How's the spreadsheet coming, Bill?"

"I haven't started on it yet, Jack, but I did take a quick look at the estimates."

"What do you think of them?"

"There's no summary of the extra work estimates, which we need before starting on the spreadsheet. As you know, for a good overview, it's a good practice to summarize the estimates for extra work. We do that for material purchases as well."

"Perhaps Brian has a summary and didn't include it in his transmission."

"Could you check on that, Jack?"

"I will. Keep me posted on your progress, will you, Bill?"

"Okay."

When Jack saw Harry, Harry said, "I haven't got much time this morning. What's on your mind, Jack?"

"Brian told me that his estimates for time extensions and impacts were rejected by the engineers when he submitted his extra work tenders."

"Does that mean the extra work was sublet to another contractor?"

"No. It means Brian accepted the price adjustment and proceeded with the work, with the proviso to issue a claim at a later date."

"That's stupid."

"Not entirely, Harry. He was probably trying to keep other contractors off his site."

"Hmm. So, what's the solution?"

"When I get to Calgary I'll check with the project manager how he kept track of the extra work. I hope the original contract work was properly isolated."

"And if it wasn't?"

"We'll have a major problem."

"What do you want me to do?"

"I just wanted you to know that we may have an additional problem that we did not anticipate."

"Jack, that's what I hired you for. I don't need to know all the details. I only want to know about fraud, gross incompetence, and major expenditures."

3

Brian Forbes called Mike Kowalski, his upgrader project manager. "Hello Mike. Harry Broughton has appointed Jack Malone to check on our impact claim for the upgrader."

"I'm glad. Jack is very knowledgeable about this type of claim."

"I know, but I just want to make sure there are no surprises. Jack has already asked for all our estimates and tender documents for the extra work."

"We have nothing to hide!"

"I know that, but he may also want to see how we tracked the extra work. How have you tracked this work?"

"It wasn't always possible to track it properly, Brian. Much of the work is intermingled with our contract work."

"That can be a problem, all right, but we could still attempt to track it somehow."

"I'll check with the foremen and let you know what we did, Brian."

"Okay. But if it wasn't completely tracked, what can be done in retrospect?"

"We could try to create a plausible record for each extra, Brian."

"Hmm. Jack may not like that. If the claim ever reaches discovery stages, you'll have to testify under oath how and when the records were established."

"Let me get back to you on that, Brian."

Jack arrived in Calgary just before noon on Monday. Brian greeted him warmly at the luggage carousel and grabbed his suitcase. They walked to the car park, got into Brian's BMW, and headed downtown to the Fairmont Palliser Hotel, where Jack checked in.

Brian was a stocky, medium-sized man with dark hair, a mustache, and a tanned complexion. He wore a leather jacket, blue jeans, a red and black-checkered shirt, and fancily carved cowboy boots—without spurs.

They settled down in The Palliser's Oak Room Lounge and ordered roast beef sandwiches and Coors Light beers.

"Did the files I sent you come through all right?" Brian enquired.

"Yes, but we didn't get an electronic summary of the extra work estimates."

"That's because we don't have one, Jack."

"Why not?"

"We didn't think we needed one."

"Well, the summary can easily be established by your estimating program. Can you see to it, Brian?"

"Sure, but why is it so important?"

"It saves us doing it in Toronto the hard way. We don't have the estimating program to do it."

"Yes, but I meant, why do you need it at all?"

"I want to compare the estimated items with the purchased items, to make sure our labor overrun is not due to estimate shortages."

"I see. You do take the task seriously, don't you?"

"No other way, Brian. We can't ask the owners to pay for our mistakes, you know. Besides, if they catch us passing on obvious mistakes to them, they'll assume the entire claim is a mistake they should reject."

"God, Jack, you know that claims are padded."

"I know. Harry wants to eliminate the practice. He thinks we'll be more successful in the long run."

"That's bullshit, and you know it, Jack. The owners will offer us half the claim amount even after we reduced it."

"They may try, but we stand a better chance to prove we're correct—if we are correct. Besides, there is a customer relations angle to consider as well. If our customers believe we are deceitful, this harms our reputation. Consequently, the success of future projects will also be in jeopardy."

"Gosh! Harry really brainwashed you, didn't he?"

"It is true that this is Harry's position, but he didn't brainwash me, as you put it. It's also my view."

"How the hell did you ever make a profit in your division, Jack?"

"I made it, believe me, Brian, the honest way."

Brian shook his head: "Beats me."

Jack was downhearted. He had assumed that Brian and he always had an excellent relationship. Now, so it seemed, they were miles apart in their thinking. He decided to try once more.

"Don't you see the value in what we're trying to do, Brian? We may not get any more for our claims financially, but we will build a better reputation for ourselves. This is important to get us short listed."

"I suppose you're right, Jack. I just detest the way these bastards treat us. Look at the way they butchered our estimates for extra work. The engineers wouldn't even negotiate with us. Chop-chop! Take it or leave it! All of our estimates for impacts on our contract work as well as other margins had disappeared. 'Do you want us to call in another contractor?' They asked, laughing at our objections. What could I do? I gave them written notice that we will submit a claim to recover our losses, that's what I did. I wanted to keep other contractors off our site, Jack. What would you have done?"

Jack nodded silently. It was a tough question. He had experienced similar treatments many times. On one occasion, he called the engineers' bluff and ended up with a non-union contractor on-site doing all the extra work. This interference had badly affected his productivity, but the owners laughed at him when he asked for some compensation. "Read your contract," they told him. "We can engage additional contractors anytime we want on this jobsite. You should have known at tender time that this might affect you, and you should've made an allowance for it in your tender. If you didn't make such an allowance, don't come crying to us now."

"I know what you're saying, Brian, but I can't give you any answers till I finish my investigation. For your own benefit and that of the company, I need your cooperation for my investigation. Can I count on that?"

"You know you can, Jack. I just wanted to let off some steam at the treatment we have so far received. Harry thinks it's a piece of cake doing these projects."

"I'm pretty sure he realizes the difficulty, Brian. That's one reason why he wants me to get involved. By the way, is there any truth to the rumor that our tender was substantially low?"

Brian swallowed a food morsel and swilled it down with some beer. "Nothing officially confirmed, Jack. The engineers didn't release the tender amounts."

"But you found out unofficially?"

"Yes, from one of our competitors—a friend of mine."

"By how much were we low?"

"About eight percent, I'm led to believe."

Jack whistled. "That's a lot! Did you compare estimate breakdowns with your friend?"

"I did."

"So where was the big difference?"

"Labor, mostly."

"But how can that be if your material amounts had little difference?"

"Must be because of the labor amount we used for the owner-supplied materials."

"Did the engineers not issue a list of those?"

"They did, but they specified that contractors had to establish their own quantities because of the uncertain design of the fast-track project, which they anticipated would change substantially—and it did, judging by the number of contract changes."

"Still, if contractors would go by the list provided for the owner-supplied materials, their labor estimates should have been very close for it."

"The problem, Jack, is that we wanted to establish a competitive edge for ourselves regarding the owner-supplied materials, and we decided to reduce the measured items provided in their list by ten percent. We know that the engineers always protect themselves in case their measurements are short. That's the reason why we were not concerned about the eight percent tender difference. Most of the other contractors probably just allowed labor for the material quantities provided in the engineers' list."

"I can believe that, Brian, but what about your friend? What did he tell you he had allowed?"

"He didn't say. As you know, most contractors, friends or no friends, shy away from divulging their labor calculation methods. My friend is no exception."

Jack nodded. He could believe that, too. He got up. "I want to freshen up, and then relax a bit. I've had a long day already."

"Well, enjoy yourself tonight. I'll have a private office ready for you tomorrow. Mary Maier, my secretary, will provide you with anything you need. I have to go to a jobsite first thing in the morning and may be late arriving at the office."

"Thanks, Brian."

4

Jack arrived at MDF's Calgary offices at eight thirty the next morning. Mary Maier showed him to his assigned office, furnished with a desk, a telephone, four armchairs, a credenza, and a meeting table. The only decoration was a twenty-four-inch print on the wall of an old North American Indian wearing a deerskin jacket. He had a feather in his hair, a tomahawk in his hands, a deeply wrinkled face, and sad, black eyes. In one corner were two bankers' boxes holding the upgrader's tender and claim documents.

Mary Maier was in her late thirties, of medium height. Her brown hair was streaked with natural blond and she had brown eyes, a light rosy complexion, and a nice figure.

"Can I get you a cup of coffee, Mr. Malone?"

"Call me Jack, please, Mary. A cup of coffee would be welcome, thanks —black, no sugar."

As Mary brought his cup of coffee he asked her, "When is Brian expected?"

"He usually comes in shortly after nine."

"What are your office hours here?"

"The estimators start at eight and usually work late. I start at 8:30, but came in early today."

"Not on my account, I hope."

She blushed and gave him a shy smile. "No, I had some catching up to do," she said awkwardly.

He smiled back at her. "Well, thanks for looking after me. When Brian comes in, please tell him to come see me."

"Will do."

Jack studied the Consortium's tender documents and MDF's original estimate for about two hours. Then Mary showed up with another cup of coffee.

"Brian just called me," she said. "He apologizes; he said he is unavoidably detained at a jobsite for most of the day."

"Thanks, Mary. Please ask Clara Goodman to come and see me for a few minutes."

"I'll check if she's available."

Clara Goodman, Brian's chief estimator, was small, good-looking woman with short brown hair and blue eyes. She knocked on Jack's open door.

Jack looked up and said, "Come in Clara. Close the door and sit down." He studied her for a few seconds and asked, "Did Brian ask you to prepare an estimate summary for the upgrader?"

"He did, but I'm presently tied up with a tender closing."

"When can I expect it, Clara?"

"I should have done by Thursday afternoon."

"Fine," he said. "Actually I want two summaries—one of the approved extra work estimates and the other one including the original estimate."

"No problem," she said.

"There is one more thing, Clara."

She looked at him expectantly.

"Brian told me that he received information that our estimated labor may be on the low side. Did you double-check your estimate to dispute the rumor?"

She hesitated before answering. "Yes, I did," she assured him.

He looked at her more sternly. "And, what did you find?"

She fumbled with a button on her blouse and said, "Our estimate checked out okay."

"Do you have any theories why our tender ended up eight percent low?"

"No," she answered, rather too quickly.

"Okay, Clara, you can get back to your tender closing. Let me have the summaries ASAP."

"Will do," she said, and rushed out of his office.

He shook his head. He had a strange feeling she was lying to him. After looking again at the estimate he closed it in disgust and decided to have an early lunch.

He found a little Hungarian restaurant two blocks from the office and ordered its goulash special. After lunch he pondered again over the estimate. He had done his own spot checks and found nothing wrong with the labor units and the extensions. So, where was the error, if any? Of course, Brian's friend could have allowed too much for his labor, but he doubted it. Competition was too keen these days. If there was a mistake in their estimate, it had to be a quantity shortage, he decided, and Bill Snider's estimate-to-purchases comparison would detect it, he hoped. He would know soon.

Back at the office, Mary told Jack that Brian phoned again to say he would not be coming to the office that day. Jack nodded and asked Mary for the phone number of Mike Kowalski, who was still at the jobsite supervising the commissioning.

Jack dialed Mike's number: "Hello Mike. This is Jack Malone. How are you?"

"Busy."

"I assume you've heard that Harry appointed me to investigate the feasibility of your claim against the Consortium?"

"Yes, I've heard. How can I help you?"

"I would like some information regarding your records procedures."

"What kind of information?"

"Well, for one thing, how did you track the extra work?"

"What do you mean by track the extra work?"

"Did you keep a record of the labor used for each of the extra work orders?"

"You've got to be kidding! Did you ever run a fast-track project, Jack?"

"I take it that you didn't keep a record, right?"

"That's right. What good would it have done?"

"Well, we could have used it to establish a norm for the overrun of labor."

"Do you have any other questions?"

"Yes. How did you keep track of the completed construction work?"

"By comparing the labor expended to the total labor estimated."

"That method is only accurate if labor does not run over, Mike."

"True, but we didn't know about an overrun."

"Well, Brian had some information to suggest this, which, I'm sure, he passed onto you."

"So, shoot me!"

"No use getting sassy, Mike. I'm trying to help you guys with your claim."

"I'm rather busy today, Jack. Do you have any more questions?"

"Not at the moment, Mike. I may come to the site to see you in the next few days."

"You're always welcome, Jack."

Jack contemplated Mike's answers for a while. None of what Mike had told him would support the claim. He could not understand how Brian's division expected the Consortium to dole out money for a major claim without supporting evidence. He knew he could convince Harry of this problem, but he also knew that Harry wanted him to find ways to arrive at a settlement with the Consortium. Jack had no idea at present how to accomplish that feat.

He finally decided to call Frank Butler, the oil Consortium's chief engineer, and asked Mary for his phone number. She gave him a slip of paper with Frank Butler's site number and his Calgary office number.

"You look concerned, Jack," she said, caringly.

"I am concerned."

"Because of your talk with Mike?"

"Yes, partially. A few things about this claim don't make sense to me, and Mike seemed too defensive."

"He's probably worried about his bonus, which depends on the claim amount."

Jack said, "MDF doesn't pay bonuses on claims, Mary."

"No, but claims go to the division's bottom line, which determines the bonuses."

"Of course. Incidentally, you gave me two phone numbers for Frank Butler. Do you know where I can reach him?"

"At the jobsite, today."

"Thanks, Mary."

"You're welcome."

Jack dialed Frank Butler's jobsite number. After three rings, a woman answered. Jack said, "My name is Jack Malone from MDF. Could you connect me with Frank Butler?"

"This is Mr. Butler's phone, but he's in a meeting at the moment."

"Please ask him to call me at MDF's Calgary office."

"I'll leave him a message."

Frank Butler called Jack about an hour later and asked, "What can I do for you, Mr. Malone?"

"Harry Broughton has appointed me to have a closer look at MDF's impact claim against the oil Consortium. Could you send me a list of Consortium-supplied materials that were charged out to MDF?"

"I think MDF kept track of them too, but, yes, I can send you our list. Give me your email address."

"Please use MDF's Calgary email address."

"Okay. Anything else?"

"No. However, I'd like to meet with you, at your convenience."

"I'll be at the jobsite until Thursday and back in my Calgary office on Friday, but I'm tied up on Friday. Call my Calgary secretary for an appointment next week."

"I will. Thanks, Mr. Butler."

Jack was still working on some documents at five thirty when Mary came to his office. "Will you be working much longer, Jack?"

"No, I'm finished for today."

"Can I drop you off at your hotel?"

"I don't want to impose on you."

"No problem. It's on my way home."

Mary was a fast but careful driver. Just before they arrived at the hotel, Jack casually asked her, "Can I treat you to dinner, Mary?"

"I'm free, but I don't want to impose on you."

"No imposition. It'll be my pleasure Mary."

"Fine. I'll park the car in the adjoining parkade."

After they settled down in the dining room, Mary ordered the pan-fried rainbow trout and a glass of Chenin Blanc and Jack ordered the filet mignon and a glass of Merlot.

Mary asked, "How long will you be in Calgary?"

"Not too long, I hope."

"Why? Don't you like Calgary?"

"I do, but my job here is short-lived."

"I suppose you'll miss your wife and children, all the same."

"I still miss my wife, but we've had no children."

"Still?" she asked.

"Yes. She died two years ago, but I still miss her."

"I'm sorry," Mary said.

"It's okay. Life must go on, as they say. Do you have family in Calgary?"

"No, my family is in Winnipeg. I live alone."

"Not married?" he enquired.

"Divorced, It's a sad story—incompatibility."

"It happens," he said.

She nodded.

"What are your general interests, Mary?" he asked, changing the subject.

"I have many interests, Jack—swimming, skating, traveling, reading, enjoying music—you name it."

"I have more or less similar interests," he said. "My problem is finding the time to enjoy them."

Having found common ground they spent two hours exploring them. Finally Mary said, "I'd better head home."

"I'll walk you to your car."

After she unlocked her car door, she turned around and gave him a peck on the cheek. "Thanks for dinner and a lovely evening, Jack," she said.

"My pleasure, entirely," he assured her.

He watched her drive down the ramp of the parkade. Did he just imagine it, or did she briefly brush his lips as she gave him the peck on the cheek? Perhaps, he thought, this is just wishful thinking on my part.

5

Jack arrived at MDF's Calgary office at nine Wednesday morning. Mary greeted him with a big smile and informed him that Brian would be in at ten thirty.

"Fine," said Jack. "Please contact Steve Hiller's secretary for me, Mary, and find out if he's free for lunch today." Steve Hiller was the lawyer Brian had hired to file MDF's claim.

Ten minutes later, Mary came to his office with a steaming cup of coffee. "Mr. Hiller will meet you for lunch at the Palliser Hotel," she informed him.

"Thanks, Mary."

Jack spent the next ninety minutes studying the claim to prepare himself for the meeting with Steve Hiller.

Brian came to his office shortly after eleven o'clock and said, "I hear you arranged a meeting with Steve Hiller."

"That's right. You're welcome to join us."

"I should hope so."

"Give me some background on the man, Brian."

"Well, what can I say? He's tall, with brown hair and blue eyes, well groomed, and a little cynical, but he knows the legal aspects of construction claims. He's quite assertive, though, and doesn't like interference. So, watch yourself, Jack."

"Listen, Brian, I'm here to investigate the claim, and if I find something wrong, I'm obligated to say so—even to your expert lawyer."

"Okay, Jack. I just wanted to warn you about his character."

Mary had reserved a table at the Rimrock Restaurant and Steve Hiller was already there when Jack and Brian arrived. He introduced Jack to his claims expert, a chap named Ken Smith. "I thought Ken might give us some details regarding the financial validity of the claim," he said.

Ken Smith was a short, stocky man with dark hair and brown eyes. He wore a brown, three-piece suit, and a light-blue shirt with a maroon-colored tie. He shook Jack's hand with a warm smile. "Glad to meet you, Mr. Malone."

"Likewise. Call me Jack, please."

The conversation over lunch centered on local and national politics. After the waiter served their coffees and brandies, Steve asked Ken to explain to them his opinion regarding the claim validity.

"Well," said Ken, "we have several methods to establish the normal productivity at a jobsite, but, in this case, only one was suitable."

"Why's that?" Jack wanted to know.

"Well, mainly because we're up against a lack of task completion tracking."

"So, what method have you used to establish the productivity norm, considering that literally all tasks were impacted by contract changes?" Jack pressed.

"The only suitable method, in our opinion, is to compare the billings with the expended labor. We think the first quarter of construction proves the norm."

"For God's sake, Ken, that's asking for trouble."

"Hold it right there, Jack," Steve demanded. He turned to Ken, "Don't say another word. I think we can excuse you. I would like to have a private talk with my clients."

Ken got up, bade them goodbye, and left.

"We cannot influence the opinion of our claims expert, Jack," Steve said sternly. "Opposing counsel will enquire about that, and if he finds out we caused a change in the claims expert's opinion, the courts will take a dim view of it."

"Well," said Jack, "the courts will take an even dimmer view of your so-called claims expert's opinion without our influence."

"Please explain to me why you don't like his way of establishing the labor norm on this site, Jack."

"There are several reasons. First, MDF had most of the materials delivered and stockpiled during the first quarter of construction. This alone would distort the billing-to-expended-labor comparison. Then our crews performed most of the simpler labor tasks during this period. And finally, I think Brian probably also overbilled the labor and materials during this period."

Steve looked at Brian, who just nodded his agreement.

"Well," said Steve, "in any case, our claims expert doesn't have another method to advance. So, we're stuck with it."

"You mean that you won't scrap it after what I've told you?"

"That's right. It's all we have to go with it."

Jack got up and turned to Brian: "Let's go. I've heard enough."

"You go ahead, Jack. I want another word with Steve."

"Suit yourself."

Jack took a taxi back to the office, phoned Harry, and informed him of his conversation with Steve Hiller and Ken Smith. "The method proposed by the claims expert of proving the validity of our claim will put our entire claim at risk, in my opinion, Harry."

"Thanks for letting me know, Jack. Give me some time to think about it. I'll get back to you on it. How's the rest of your investigation coming?"

"I think I'll have something to report to you next Monday, or Tuesday, at the latest."

"Look forward to it, Jack."

That evening, Mary offered Jack another ride and he invited her for dinner again. After dinner, as they walked out of the dining room, Mary turned to Jack and asked, "Your place or mine?"

Jack gave her a surprised look. "Let's go into the lounge for a nightcap," he said. They ordered Kahlúas. After they received their drinks, Jack said, "Harry frowns upon relationships between his employees, Mary."

"How would he know about it? Even if he did, we're mature, consenting adults whose private lives should be of no concern to him," she said.

"He may see our jobs as being in conflict—you having to be loyal to Brian, and me having to be loyal to him," Jack pointed out.

"I do not believe we would let our private lives interfere with our divided loyalties, Jack."

He gave her a searching look and finished his Kahlúa. "I agree with you," he said. "Finish your drink. We'll make it my place—it's more convenient."

She just smiled.

They were barely inside his room when she put her arms around his neck and gave him a lingering and passionate kiss. Her exploring tongue inside his mouth aroused him immediately. He said, "I have to take a quick shower, Mary."

"Me, too," she said, "I'll join you."

After they toweled each other off, they kissed again, and Jack put his hand between Mary's legs. He stroked her gently, and Mary groaned softly with pleasure. "Let's go to bed," she suggested.

In bed they continued their passionate kiss. Then, Mary cupped her hand over Jack's erection and rubbed its juice over it in a circular motion while Jack continued to stroke her gently. Both were very adept at foreplay. They groaned softly and kissed each other eagerly.

After what seemed like forever, Mary suddenly stopped her circular hand motion and quickly guided his erection into her. By this time Jack was fully aroused and pushed it in to the limit. Mary, gripped by a convulsing orgasm, let out an ecstatic scream, while Jack ejaculated forcefully, groaning "ah...ah...ah," until fully spent. They remained coupled and embraced for almost half an hour, kissing each other gratefully.

Finally Mary said, "I better get dressed."

"Why?" he wanted to know.

"I have to drive home," she said.

"No need," Jack insisted. "Stay here."

"But I have no toothbrush and pajamas along," she complained.

"I have an extra toothbrush in my bag, and you can have one of my shirts for cover," he assured her. "I'll get room service to bring us an early breakfast."

"No more fooling around while I'm sleeping," she insisted, giving up.

"I'm not sure if I can promise that," he laughed.

Facing each other over toast, scrambled eggs, and orange juice the next morning, she gave him an admiring look.

"You're quite a lover boy," she said.

He got up, walked around the table, and gave her a gentle kiss. "Mary, you were fantastic last night," he said, "but remember what I told you in the lounge. Be careful that you don't betray your feelings at the office."

She laughed. "On one condition," she said.

"What's that?" he asked, alarmed.

"That you promise me a repeat performance."

"You're on," he assured her.

6

Jack requested a brief meeting with Brian on Thursday morning.

"I might as well tell you, Brian,. So far I'm not impressed with any part of your claim and how you arrived at it. I'm not impressed with Mike's record keeping, I'm not impressed with your claims expert's method of proving our production loss, I'm not impressed with your legal counsel's stubborn attitude, and I'm not impressed with your lack of determining the cause of your abnormally low tender."

Brian gave him a worried look. "What do you suggest we do, Jack?"

"That's up to Harry. I'm going to report what I found to him on Monday and he can tell us how he wants to proceed."

"Yes, but how would you proceed?"

"I don't know, Brian. I think I would withdraw the present claim and negotiate a settlement with the Consortium."

"That's easier said than done, Jack. Frank Butler is a prime asshole!"

"Well, we may have to go over his head."

"I've tried that, without success."

"Who is the Consortium's top guy in charge of this upgrader?"

"A fellow by the name of Humphrey Paulson. He's the Alberta VP."

"Do we have any background info on him?"

"Not much."

"I'll ask Harry if he can get us a brief career history on him."

Jack headed back to his newly found Hungarian restaurant for lunch and was brooding silently over a cup of coffee. He expected Clara's extra work summary that afternoon and he doubted if Bill Snider would find any big discrepancies. Clara had a well-known reputation for accuracy. In any case, he could not accomplish much more in Calgary and he seriously considered flying back to Toronto next week.

Jack met with Clara at four o'clock. She gave him a hard copy of the extra work summary, plus an electronic version on a flash drive.

Jack looked at the hard copy and asked, "What about a combined file including our original estimate?"

Clara looked at him nervously and said, "I've encountered a problem creating it."

"What kind of a problem?"

"I'm getting a message that says 'incompatible.'"

"That doesn't make sense, Clara. You didn't get such a message for all the extra work estimates, did you?"

"No," she said. "I'll have to look into it some more."

"Do that," he told her. Then he sent an email to Bill Snider with the electronic copy attached. He asked Bill to give him his comparison results ASAP.

7

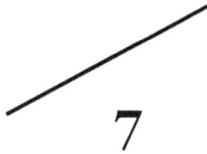

As Jack arrived at the office on Friday, Mary told him that Bill Snider had already called for him. When Jack returned Bill's call, Bill told him that he has a problem merging the original estimate with the extra work estimates summary.

Jack said, "Clara has the same problem. I've thought about it last night, and I have an idea how to fix it. I only want a material-estimate-to-purchases comparison from you, Bill. Why don't you zero out the labor-units column, and try merging the files? Let me know if it works."

"Okay."

Bill called him back shortly after lunch. "I have good news and bad news for you, Jack. Which do you want first?"

"Give me the good news."

"Well, we found very few discrepancies between the estimated and purchased quantities – hardly worth mentioning."

This may be good news for an accountant like Bill, but it was bad news for Jack. He would have to look further for possible labor mistakes.

"And what's the bad news?" he asked.

"My assistant ran into something peculiar while zeroing out the labor units."

"What's that?"

"The labor units in the extra work estimates summary for Consortium-supplied—length materials like pipe and cable—are more than three times higher than for the same materials in the original estimate."

Jack blew a low whistle. This could be what he was looking for. "I'll have to look into that. Thanks for your help, Bill."

"You're welcome. Enjoy your weekend."

"Thanks. You, too, Bill. I'll see you when I get back."

Jack sat back and contemplated Bill's "bad news" for a while. He felt he was close to a solution but he needed Clara's input. He called Mary.

"Mary, please ask Clara to come to my office."

"I'll see if she's available."

As Clara knocked on his open door Jack said, "Come in, Clara. Close the door and sit down."

She did, giving him a nervous look.

"Clara," he said, "I have a report from head office that the labor units for the length items of the Consortium-supplied materials are about three times higher in your extra work estimate summary than in your original estimate. Can you explain that to me?"

She looked horrified and started to sob.

"Stop bawling," he told her, "and answer my question."

She looked up at him, teary-eyed, and said, "I've made an awful mistake, Mr. Malone."

"Tell me about it."

"When I entered the list of Consortium-supplied materials into our computer, I neglected to convert their metric units into imperial units—meters into feet. Our computer program is set up for imperial units."

He blew another low whistle. "Let me get this straight," he said. "For each meter of pipe or cable, then, you should have entered three point three times as much in feet?"

"Three point twenty-eight times," she corrected him.

Of course. He remembered one of his teachers telling him that a kilometer is about 2,000 feet shorter than a mile. That would make it about 3,280 feet long.

"So, for each thousand meters of measured items in the Consortium's material list you should have entered 3,280 feet in your computer."

"Yes, except for our ten-percent reduction."

"When did you discover your mistake?"

"After tender closing. Brian asked me to double-check all labor units, because one of his competitor friends had told him that our labor allowance is low."

"Did you tell Brian about the mistake?"

"Yes, but he told me to forget it. We needed the work and he was sure we could recover the loss through extra work orders."

"Did you also determine the dollar amount of your error?"

"Yes, it was close to the eight percent our tender was low."

He nodded, feeling strangely satisfied. At least this explained the labor-shortage mystery. However, what annoyed him is that Brian could have easily withdrawn his tender prior to acceptance by the Consortium, since their specifications did not demand a firm tender for a specified period.

"Okay, Clara," he said, with a deeply burdened sigh, "that's all for now."

She got up and gave him another pleading look. "I'm truly sorry, Mr. Malone," she uttered, quickly leaving and closing the door behind her.

Jack sighed again. He liked Brian, but he knew that Harry would be upset enough to fire him.

After a few minutes, he put two files into his briefcase and left the office, saying goodbye only to Mary. He decided to walk all the way back to his hotel to clear his mind.

After he took a hot bath to relax he phoned Harry to give him a detailed report. Harry listened silently and patiently without interrupting Jack. When Jack finished his report Harry said, "I'm flying out on Monday. Meet me at the Palliser Hotel for lunch."

Jack decided to rent a car and drive out to Banff for the weekend. Perhaps some relaxation in the hot springs would help him concentrate on how to proceed with this claim.

8

Jack stayed in his room on Monday morning studying the files he had taken along on Friday. Just before noon he went down to the Rimrock Restaurant where he waited for Harry to join him. Harry arrived at twelve thirty.

"Sorry," Harry said. "My flight was delayed."

After they placed their orders for lunch, Harry told Jack that he had arranged to meet with Brian and Clara after two o'clock. "I've also arranged to meet with Steve Hiller at three thirty," he added.

During lunch Harry asked, "What do you do for excitement in Calgary, Jack?"

"I don't really know. I spent the weekend in Banff."

"Banff? That's in the mountains."

"Yes, with good hot springs. It helped me to relax and think about how to proceed with this claim."

"Have you come to any conclusions?"

"Not yet. I was going to discuss some possibilities with you, Harry."

"Let's wait till after my meetings this afternoon."

When they arrived at MDF's Calgary office, Harry greeted Mary warmly and said, "Ask Brian to come to the boardroom, will you?"

Brian tried to be jovial as he shook hands with Harry, but Harry's demeanor remained cool. However, to relax Brian Harry asked him a few questions about his construction in progress.

Then he said, "You have made several mistakes regarding the upgrader tender and the claim against the Consortium, Brian."

Brian didn't deny it. He just nodded.

"Your first mistake was to let the tender stand without consulting with me, knowing you would experience a loss."

A tinge of red crept into Brian's cheeks, but he remained silent.

"Your second mistake was to file a claim against the Consortium that included the loss, for which you were responsible."

This time, Brian objected. "We always pad claims, Harry," he said.

Harry nodded. "But not to this extent, Brian."

Brian face got a little redder.

"Your third mistake," Harry continued, "was to hire a lawyer who is willing to deceive our customer along with you, Brian."

This time, Brian got up, red with anger, and asked, "Is that all, Harry?"

"Not quite," Harry said calmly. "Sit down Brian. Your worst mistake was when you lied to Jack. Jack is my representative, and lying to him is the same as lying to me. I can't have that. You're fired. Pack your things and get out."

Brian walked out of the boardroom without another word. As he passed Jack's office he stopped and said, "Thanks for nothing, 'friend!'"

Brian drove straight home. He opened the door and called out to his wife, "I'm home, Katherine."

She came out of the kitchen and gave him a worried look. He was usually home much later. "Are you all right, Brian?" She asked him.

"Yeah, as all right as a man can be who just got fired," he said as he headed for the liquor cabinet and poured himself two shots of bourbon.

"What happened?" she asked anxiously.

"I've made a mistake and Harry didn't like it. That's what happened," he said and drank half his bourbon.

"It must have been quite a mistake," offered Katherine.

"No worse than other mistakes in construction," said Brian, finishing his drink. "Except this time I lied about it."

"You lied to Harry?"

"No, no. I lied to Jack Malone. Harry appointed him to investigate the validity of financial claims against our customers."

"So, how did Harry find out about your lie?" Katherine wanted to know.

Brian poured himself another drink and said, "Jack reported it to Harry. He could have covered for me, but decided Harry should know."

"I don't understand that, Brian. You and Jack were always such good friends!"

"Yeah, well friendship doesn't mean much to Jack in his new position, I guess."

"Where is Jack staying in Calgary?"

"The Fairmont Palliser Hotel," said Brian, and sat back brooding.

Katherine went into their bedroom and closed the door. She called information for the phone number of the Fairmont Palliser Hotel and asked to be connected, then she asked for Jack Malone's room. There was no answer, and she decided to call back later.

Back at the office Harry phoned Mary and asked her to send in Clara.

Clara entered the boardroom with red eyes. She had obviously been crying. Harry told her to sit down.

"You have made some mistakes regarding the upgrader tender, Clara," Harry started.

"I'm so sorry," she sobbed.

"Mistakes happen," Harry continued, "and I can excuse your neglect to convert the Consortium's metric dimensions to imperial ones. However, you also lied to Jack Malone, trying to cover up your mistake. Mr. Malone is my representative, and lying to him is the same as lying to me. I can't have that, Clara."

She rubbed the tears from her eyes. "I wanted to remain loyal to Brian," she said softly. "I promise this will never happen again, Mr. Broughton," she added.

He gave her a long and tender look. He knew she was by far one of MDF's best estimators, and this conversion neglect was her first major mistake, as far as he knew.

"Okay," he told her firmly, "I'll only give you a stern warning this time. If it happens again, I'll have to dismiss you."

"Thanks, Mr. Broughton," she looked at him with relief. "You won't regret it."

"I hope so," he said. "Now get back to work."

Then he called Mary. "Mary, please ask Tom Sweeny to come to the boardroom."

Tom was one of MDF's senior project managers, a tall, lanky chap, with grey hair, grey eyes, a deep tan, casual dress, and a firm handshake. "How do you do, Harry? Good to see you again," he said.

"Good to see you, too, Tom. Please sit down."

Harry poured himself a glass of water. "Tom," he began, "I've had to dismiss Brian this afternoon and I want you to take charge here, temporarily, until I find a replacement. Is that okay with you?"

"It's okay as long as it's just temporary. You know my forte is project management, Harry."

"I know. I hope to find a suitable replacement ASAP."

"Anything special you want me to look after?"

"Just the routine management. Jack Malone will look after the claim against the Consortium."

"I hope you don't mind my calling you if I run up against something unusual."

"Please do. Now, if you'll excuse me, I'll have to run along. I have an appointment with Brian's legal beagle."

Harry stopped briefly at Jack's office and said, "Let's go, Jack. Our taxi is waiting."

They arrived at Steve Hiller's office right on time, but Mr. Hiller kept them waiting for ten minutes, which annoyed Harry. Mr. Hiller finally showed up and greeted them with a foolish smile.

"I'm sorry for the delay, gentlemen, please follow me to our boardroom."

After they sat down Steve Hiller said, "You wanted a meeting, Mr. Broughton?"

"Yes. I'll make it short. Jack Malone brought to your attention his objection to your claims expert's proposal of proving MDF's productivity loss, but you insist on going ahead with it, despite the explanations Mr. Malone gave you."

"I merely want us to be in the best position to convince the courts of the financial validity of your claim."

"Mr. Hiller, we engaged you to protect the legal aspects of our claim, not to find ways to deceive our customer and the courts. That's not MDF's way of doing business. I'm afraid I'll have to dismiss you."

Steve Hiller looked shocked. "What about the claim?" he wanted to know.

"That's no longer your concern," said Harry, getting up. "Send us your final account."

"If that's what you want."

"That's what I want," said Harry and walked out.

Jack followed him.

In the taxi on the way to the hotel Jack asked, "How do you want to proceed with the claim, Harry?"

"Let's discuss it after dinner, Jack."

After freshening up in their rooms they met again in the Rimrock Restaurant. Both ordered a New York steak and a glass of Merlot for dinner.

"Are you planning any yachting trips, Harry?" Jack wanted to know.

"Yes, I'm getting ready for a trip to P.E.I."

"I wish I'd have the time for that."

"Time shouldn't be a problem with your new job, Jack. You'll have lots of time between claims."

"Looking after a yacht takes time, too."

"You don't have to buy one. There are plenty for rent."

"Oh, I didn't know that."

After they finished their steaks they ordered coffee and brandies and Jack said, "How do you want to proceed with the claim, Harry?"

"Well, not with the help of any lawyers and the courts."

"What do you have in mind?"

"I want you to contact the Consortium and offer to withdraw the claim. Tell them we want to negotiate a settlement with them."

"Brian dealt with their chief engineer, a chap by the name of Frank Butler. He said this fellow has a biased attitude towards MDF."

"Go right to the top if you have to. Engineers are often overprotective."

"With Brian's padding removed, our four point five million dollar claim could end up at less than half that amount."

"I'm aware of that, Jack. We're still better off to negotiate a settlement."

Back in his hotel room at ten o'clock, Jack settled in an easy chair to continue reading a Len Deighton novel when his phone rang. He picked it up, thinking that Harry wanted to add something to his instructions.

"Hello."

Silence.

"Hello?"

More silence. Then, "How could you do this to your friend, Jack?" He recognized Brian's wife Katherine's voice.

"He admired you. I looked up to you, and so did our son. How could you do this to him! How can you live with

yourself after this treachery? Can you even sleep at night?"
She hung up before Jack could answer.

Jack closed his book. He remembered the time he had
first met Katherine and their son at one of MDF's management meetings. They'd had a great time and even played
some games together.

9

The following morning Jack phoned Frank Butler. After the essential introductions he said, "Mr. Butler, MDF is considering withdrawing its claim and entering into settlement negotiations with you. Can we meet and discuss this?"

"Your claim should never have been filed in the first place, Mr. Malone, and I'm not interested in any settlement negotiations. You don't have a valid claim."

"Is that your final word, Mr. Butler?"

"That's my final word."

Next, Jack phoned Humphrey Paulson's office. A woman with a deep and pleasant voice answered, "Mr. Paulson's office."

"My name is Jack Malone, MDF's Vice President of Customer Relations. I would like to arrange a meeting with Mr. Paulson."

"Just a moment, please."

He waited two minutes and the woman came back and said, "Mr. Paulson can see you on Thursday at three o'clock. Does that work for you?"

"It does. Thank you very much."

At eleven thirty Jack asked Mary to join him for lunch. They walked to the Hungarian restaurant. Both ordered a glass of Merlot and the Hungarian goulash special.

"I've had a call from Katherine last night, Mary." Jack said sadly.

"Brian's wife?"

"Yes."

"I gather this was an unpleasant call?"

"That's putting it mildly, Mary. I knew this job was going to get me into trouble. I should've never accepted it. Investigating inflated construction claims entails exposing some of MDF's division managers to criticism, perhaps even dismissals, and that's what happened to Brian. Dismissals may be justified, but they will surely lose me some friends."

"Do you think Brian's dismissal was justified, Jack?"

"I don't think so, but Harry thought so."

"On what basis did Harry decide this?"

"Harry did not confide his reason to me. It could be because of Brian's costly mistake."

"Gosh, Jack, employees make mistakes all the time. If you fired them for their mistakes, you wouldn't have many employees left."

"I guess I'll eventually find out from Harry what his reason was. Brian also lied to me."

"And you told Harry that Brian lied to you."

"Yes. What else could I have done?"

"Perhaps you should have anticipated a lie and convinced Brian to come clean. Harry may have given him another chance. Brian is a good manager, Jack."

Jack looked at her with surprise. This woman may well have the answer to his dilemma. He took another sip of his wine and said, "Well, it's water under the bridge, I suppose?"

"It doesn't have to be final, Jack."

"What are you suggesting?"

"Why don't you give Brian a call and apologize for what happened and offer to help him."

"Hmm. Let me think about it. Thanks for your advice, Mary."

"You're welcome, Jack. You're very good at the technical and tactical aspects of your job, but you need to spend a little more time on the moral aspects of it."

He gave her an admiring look.

Back at the office, Jack wasted no time calling Brian: "Jack, here, Brian. I just want you to know how sorry I am for what happened yesterday. I had no idea that Harry planned to take such drastic action. If there is anything I can do to help you, a good reference, or whatever, please let me know."

There was silence for a few seconds. Then Brian said, "Do me a favor, Jack."

"Certainly, Brian, what is it?"

"Drop dead!"

Jack spent the next two days taking a closer look at the extra construction work estimates and tenders.

Thursday afternoon he arrived at the Consortium's offices a few minutes early. A tall blonde, immaculately dressed in a light-grey suit, probably the woman who made his appointment, said amiably, "Sit down, please, Mr. Malone. Mr. Paulson will be with you shortly."

Right at three o'clock Humphrey Paulson came out of his office. He was a slender man, just under six feet tall with dark-brown slightly balding hair, brown eyes, a tanned face, and elegantly dressed in a dark-brown, single-breasted suit, black shoes, and a light-brown shirt with a silk tie with a floral outline on a maroon background. His only ornaments were a golden Rolex wristwatch, a golden wedding ring, and a golden tiepin. A smart-looking man, Jack observed—and probably smart, too.

He shook Jack's hand. "Mr. Malone, I presume." Jack nodded and followed him into his office.

It was a large office with a golden-colored, deep-pile carpet. The two outside walls consisted of floor-to-ceiling windows, each framing a beautiful view of the river valley. Two brown leather sofas, a mahogany coffee table, and three brown leather armchairs occupied a corner next to the windows. At the wall near the door stood a mahogany desk with another brown leather armchair with a picture of an oil refinery—probably a refinery built by the Consortium—behind it. On the fourth wall were a long mahogany credenza and a large oil painting of a mountain river, complete with fisherman casting a fly.

Humphrey Paulson sat down on one of the sofas and pointed to the other one. "Sit down, Mr. Malone."

Seeing Jack looking fondly at the oil painting he asked, "Are you a fly-fisherman, Mr. Malone?"

"Yes, I love it."

"Where do you do most of your fly-fishing?"

"Mostly in British Columbia, but also in the foothills of Alberta."

"Oh? Which rivers?"

"The Wildhay, the McLeod, the North Ram, the Brazeau, and also the Bow River, occasionally."

"I've fished in these rivers as well, except the Wildhay River, but I find the trout fish rather small in them."

"They also have larger trout, if you know how to find and fish them."

"And how do you find and fish them, if I may ask you?"

"Well, to find them, I look for deep pools in the river, also large boulders, and to fish them I have found that larger trout tend to jump out of the water to catch a fly. So, I cast my flies in such a way that when the leader rolls it out and it almost reaches the water level, I retrieve it and cast it again, often three or four times, until I entice the big ones to jump out of the water to catch the fly. The trick is to never allow the fly to land on the water, otherwise you catch too many small ones."

"That's very interesting, indeed. I'll have to try it sometimes."

"It takes a little practice, but don't give up."

They talked a good twenty minutes about their fishing experiences. Jack told Mr. Paulson a story how he once escaped an angry grizzly bear, anxious to protect her cubs, along the North Ram River.

"That sounds scary," said Mr. Paulson. "How did you manage to escape her?"

"Well, I left all my belongings behind, including my fishing rod, and waded across the river posthaste. She decided to stick with her cubs and didn't follow me, thank goodness!"

They sat for a minute in contemplation. Then, Mr. Paulson said, "I could talk all afternoon about fishing, but you came here for another purpose, Mr. Malone."

"Yes, my mission is simple: I'm here to tell you that MDF wants to withdraw its claim and negotiate a settlement with the Consortium."

"The Consortium would welcome that," said Mr. Paulson, "as long as we reach a fair settlement."

"I hate unfairness myself, Mr. Paulson. What do you consider to be a fair settlement, if I may ask?"

Mr. Paulson looked at Jack speculatively. "You don't expect me to outline the makings of a fair claim for you, do you, Mr. Malone?"

"I'm just interested in your concept of 'fair,' Mr. Paulson."

Paulson looked at him for a few seconds, sighed, and said, "It appears to us that MDF's claim was based on an impact calculation intended for all labor of the entire contract. However, since we issued the extra work orders throughout construction, the impact would have only affected half the labor, on average."

Jack was sincerely surprised. This man certainly knew his business. They looked at each other for a minute. Finally Jack said, "Let me do some number crunching and I'll get back to you. Can we arrange another meeting?"

"Certainly, Mr. Malone. My secretary manages my schedule. She'll arrange the meeting for you."

10

Jack obtained a meeting time of ten o'clock for the following Tuesday morning from Mr. Paulson's secretary. Then he headed straight back to his hotel and phoned Harry.

"Hello Harry. I've had a meeting this afternoon with Humphrey Paulson, the Consortium's Alberta VP. The meeting went well and I believe they are ready to compensate us for our impact at fifty percent of our claim."

"That's great, Jack."

"He also gave me a clue as to how they arrived at that figure, and I think I can convince him to up it."

"Be careful, Jack. We don't want to give them more impressions that we want to be paid for our own mistakes."

"What I have in mind is to create a spreadsheet using Mr. Paulson's own formula, which he gave me this afternoon. This way, I believe I can convince him to support our figures."

"How does your formula differ from his?"

"The way he arrived at his fifty percent is by using the number of extra work orders, which were issued constantly throughout construction, but he's ignoring the dollar amounts of the change orders, which were much higher during the first half of construction than during the last half. By using the dollar-weighting of extra work orders during the first half of construction, we'll end up closer to sixty percent, I hope."

"If you can accomplish this, you'll get a bonus."

Jack laughed. "I could also boost this percentage further if I added the impact of new change orders on unfinished change orders."

"I wouldn't do that, Jack. It may turn them off enough to reject the entire claim. Remember that with a fast-track construction project they could point out that we should have anticipated extra work orders, and, along with them, impacts to our original work."

"You're right, Harry. I'll just apply extra work order dollar weightings to the impact figures."

"Okay. Keep me informed."

The next morning at the office Jack asked Clara to come and see him. After she sat down he said, "I hope you're not too busy, Clara. I need a fast job done."

"I have some time in the next few days. What do you have in mind, Mr. Malone?"

"I need a spreadsheet with all the upgrader's extra work orders, and the impacts they caused to our original contract labor."

"Can you give me more details?"

"Yes. We need at least seven columns: one for the change order number; one with the approval date of the change order; one with the dollar amount of labor of the change order; one with the estimated dollar amount of labor of the original contract; one with the approved percentage of impact; one with the remaining percentage of estimated labor of the original contract; and, finally, one column containing the impact amount, which an Excel spreadsheet formula will establish. Any questions?"

Clara, who had been taking notes, said, "How do I determine the percentage of remaining labor at each change order approval date?"

"On this project we've had a steady labor force. Therefore, you can take the ratio of the remaining workdays at each extra work order approval date to the total workdays of construction, excluding the present commissioning days."

"I see. And what is the formula for the impact amounts?"

"You take the ratio of the change order labor to the estimated original contract labor, times fifteen percent, the approved impact percentage, times the percentage of the remaining labor, times the estimated original contract labor. Any more questions?"

"No, I think I've got it."

"Well, I have a question. When do you think you can complete this spreadsheet for me?"

"Probably sometime on Monday."

"Good," he said. "You can leave a message for me at the Palliser Hotel if you need my help before Monday."

Jack decided to have an early lunch at his favorite Hungarian restaurant, and then map out a negotiating strategy in a relaxed atmosphere at the hotel's lounge. Later that day, he rented a car and drove to Banff for the weekend.

When Jack arrived back at the office on Monday Clara gave him three bound copies of the spreadsheet he had requested. She must have been working the weekend.

He thanked her and inquired if she'd had any problems putting it together. She assured him she didn't have any.

He spent some time spot-checking her figures and after lunch he headed back to his hotel.

When Jack arrived on time Tuesday morning, the secretary showed him right into Humphrey Paulson's office. Mr. Paulson greeted him warmly. Jack handed him a copy of the bound, six-page spreadsheet. Both men sat down at the coffee table and the secretary brought in a tray with a coffee pot, cups, cream, and sugar. She poured them both a cup of coffee and left.

Mr. Paulson opened the brochure and started to study the various data in the spreadsheet. Occasionally, he checked some figures with a hand-held calculator, uttered "hmm-hmm," and turned the page. Jack, to avoid watching him, pretended to study his copy of the spreadsheet.

After about forty minutes, Mr. Paulson looked up and said, "The total impact is higher than I had expected, but I cannot fault the calculations. I'm prepared to recommend a settlement on the basis of this spreadsheet to my board of directors, Mr. Malone."

Jack was surprised. He had expected negotiations. "Thank you, Mr. Paulson," he said, "How do you want me to proceed?"

"Send me a letter canceling your previous claim and proposing a settlement amount based on this spreadsheet and attach the spreadsheet. However, do not head your letter up 'without prejudice,' because my board won't approve it."

"Okay, I'll have it delivered this afternoon."

"Good."

"One more thing," said Jack, on the way out.

"What's that?" Mr. Paulson enquired.

"Can I report to Harry Broughton, MDF's president, that MDF will remain on the Consortium's preferred-bidders list?"

"Certainly, Mr. Malone, we like MDF's work."

"Thank you very much, Mr. Paulson."

Jack spent the afternoon drafting the letter. Mary typed it and, after he signed it, had it delivered to Humphrey Paulson's office.

Jack cleaned his desk, put some papers into his brief-case, and headed out of his office. He decided to fly back to Toronto in the morning and give Harry the good news personally.

On the way out he told Mary that he was flying back to Toronto in the morning and invited her to join him for dinner that evening. She accepted and offered to drive him to the hotel. In the car he told her about Brian's reaction to his peace offering. She advised him not to underestimate its effect on Brian. "Dividends accrue and are paid later. The same applies to rewards for kindness," she said.

"You're amazing, Mary. Where did you acquire your philosophy?"

"From my parents, I suppose."

Waiting for their food in the hotel restaurant, they sipped their drinks quietly. Separation sadness affected each of them. Eventually Mary said softly, "I know I have no claim on you, Jack, but I'll miss you awfully."

"Likewise," he said. "What are your future plans?"

"I don't know, but I probably won't stay with MDF."

"Why?"

"I like to pick the people with whom I have to work, and I may not like Brian's replacement."

"Hmm," he said. "Perhaps the replacement will be more likeable than Brian."

She shrugged her shoulders.

"Don't you need a private secretary, Jack?"

"It hasn't occurred to me. I usually work with the divisions' secretaries. I suppose there is an advantage working with a steady. What did you have in mind?"

"I'm offering my services to you—and not just in bed."

"How about the extensive travel required?"

"I told you, I love traveling."

He gave her an approving look and said, "Let me run it past Harry. I'm sure I can convince him of the advantages."

She smiled, thinking of more than just work.

They spent another orgasmic night together in his room, and, after breakfast, she drove him to the airport.

"Bye, Lover Boy," she smiled.

He leaned over and kissed her gently on the lips.

"Bye, Fantastic," he said admiringly. "See you soon, I hope."

11

Jack had arranged a meeting with Harry for Thursday morning. Harry knew that Jack had settled MDF's claim against the Consortium and wanted the details, which Jack gave him.

"You have certainly earned your bonus, Jack," Harry conceded.

"I would like to ask you for a favor, Harry," Jack said.

"Shoot."

"You have met Mary Maier in Calgary."

Harry nodded.

"She knows her business and I would like her to help me with our claims."

"You mean accompany you to the divisions?"

"Yes."

Harry gave him a searching look and said, "You've got the hots for her, haven't you Jack?"

Jack was surprised, but didn't show it. Was Harry applying his intuition, or did he know more than he let on? "I like her very much, Harry," he said. "I may even propose marriage to her. Would you object to that?"

"Not at all, Jack. I may even offer my services as your best man. However, traveling with you to the various divisions is ineffective. You're better off to use the divisions' secretaries."

"I want to make sure we won't lose her, Harry. I believe she may not remain with the Alberta Division."

"Hmm. Okay, I'll get Fiona to suggest a transfer to Toronto to Mary. Fiona can always use more help. Besides, she will probably assign Mary to your work."

"Thanks, Harry, I'll appreciate that, and, I'm sure, Mary will, too."

Jack called Mary in the afternoon. "How're you doing, Fantastic?"

"Fine, Lover Boy."

"I talked to Harry about your accompanying me on my trips to MDF's divisions, but he doesn't like the idea. He says using the divisions' secretaries is more effective."

"He's probably right, Jack."

"I think so, too. However, he'll get Fiona to suggest a transfer to Toronto to you, and there's a good chance that Fiona will assign you to my work."

"I like that," said Mary.

"Me, too. I miss you already."

"What do you think I've been doing in the past two days?"

Jack laughed. What a woman!

12

Harry called Jack from the Yacht Club. "Jack, are you free for lunch today?"

"I am."

"Please join me at the Yacht Club at one o'clock."

"Will do."

After they placed their lunch orders, Harry said, "I think we have a problem with our new Instrumentation Division out west, Jack."

MDF had purchased an instrumentation company from a chap called Charles Bourdain. Harry thought it would give MDF more expertise than it would with merely hired trade's people to do the instrumentation work. Charles Bourdain had agreed to stay on and manage the company as an MDF division.

"What seems to be the problem?" Jack wanted to know.

"For the past three months I was getting revised profit-and-loss statements, with unsatisfactory answers to my inquiries."

"For which projects do they have contracts at the moment?"

"They're working on at least a dozen projects, but the largest one is the upgrader for the Consortium."

Jack gave a low whistle. "They may have similar problems with extra work orders as our Alberta Division had."

"That's possible, but Charles Bourdain isn't communicating this to me."

"He may not want to appear incapable of handling the situation."

"Well, I cannot allow the company to keep losing money because of some manager's misplaced vanity."

"What is it you want me to do, Harry?"

"I want you to fly out to Edmonton and investigate the problem. Report to me as soon as possible. The situation may require drastic action on my part."

"Okay, Harry, but send Charles a letter of explanation giving me some authority to look at his documents."

Jack arrived at the Edmonton International Airport at eleven and Charles Bourdain picked him up and drove him to the MacDonald Hotel where they had a lunch together.

During lunch Charles enquired, "To what do I owe the honor of your visit, Jack?"

"Harry is concerned about your recent losses, Charlie, and he wants me to investigate the reasons behind them."

"I told him not to worry. We're up against a few minor problems at the upgrader that we're trying to resolve. I don't appreciate his meddling attitude, Jack."

"You can't blame him for wanting more details when he's subsidizing your division, Charlie."

"There won't be any subsidy once we get things straightened around, Jack."

"That's what I'm here to find out, Charlie. Don't take it so personally."

"How do you want me to take it, Jack? The man obviously does not trust me to run a show that I have run successfully for many years."

Jack thought, "You don't trust him either, Charlie, otherwise you would have given him more details about your problems to satisfy him."

"Well," Jack said, "I'll just confirm a few details regarding your operation and the projects you're working on and then I'll be out of your hair, Charlie."

"Hmm. Look, I'm in meetings most of tomorrow, so I'll instruct Joe Kaluzniak, my superintendent, to assist you."

"Thanks, Charlie."

Jack met up with Joe Kaluzniak at the Instrumentation Division's office the next morning at eight thirty. Joe gave him a warm welcome and enquired, "How can I assist you, Mr. Malone?"

"To start with, I need the instrumentation tender and contract documents for the upgrader. And call me Jack."

"Okay, but it will take me a few minutes to assemble the documents, Jack. You can use the boardroom if you like."

"Thanks, Joe."

Jack sat down in the small boardroom and took a notepad from his briefcase. Celina, Charlie's secretary, brought him a cup of coffee and said, "Do you take cream and sugar, Mr. Malone?"

"No, thanks, Celina, and call me Jack, please."

Celina and Jack exchanged a few pleasantries until Joe entered with a banker's box full of documents. Jack scanned the documents until eleven thirty and decided the documents were essentially similar to the ones he had checked for Brian's claim. Then he called Joe and enquired if there was a restaurant nearby. Joe told him he liked a restaurant called Between Friends and offered to drive him there. Jack accepted the offer and invited Joe to join him for lunch.

Between Friends, situated in a round building in Southeast Edmonton, served mostly western foods. Jack and Joe ordered steak sandwiches.

Jack enquired, "Are you experiencing any particular problems at the upgrader, Joe?"

"We've had our estimates for extra work orders criticized more than usual."

"Who were you dealing with from the Consortium?"

"Their chief engineer, a chap called Frank Butler."

"Hmm," Jack mumbled. This was the same guy who gave Brian Forbes a hard time. "I'd like to take a look at your extra work order estimates, Joe."

"I'll give you the file when we get back."

"Did any of your extra work orders affect your original contract work?"

"Not really, except one, for which I'm preparing an estimate at the moment."

"How does that one affect your original work?"

"We literally have to relocate most of the instruments we have already installed because of some engineering error."

"You should watch your labor estimate for that one, Joe."

"I am. However, they are pressuring me to submit my estimate ASAP. The work is holding up their commissioning."

"Don't submit it until I've had a look at it, Joe."

"Okay, Jack."

Jack spent all afternoon looking over Joe's extra work estimates. He detected several flaws that were costing the company money. For some reason, Harry had not insisted that the Instrumentation Division replace its system with MDF's system. MDF's system made sure that incidental charges did not fall between the cracks based on the theory that if you don't list it, you won't be paid for it. He would have to talk to Harry about the oversight of exchanging the Instrumentation Division's system with MDF's system.

Furthermore, Jack found quite a few estimates that the Consortium had cut back, without vigorous objections from the Instrumentation Division—at least not in writing. Jack called Joe and asked him to come to the boardroom.

"Why did you allow the Consortium to reduce your extra work estimates, Joe?"

"We objected, naturally, Jack, but we eventually agreed because we thought we had a sufficient buffer in the estimates to withstand these cutbacks."

"Hmm," Jack murmured. "I think you may have been better advised to put your objections in writing, with the proviso to submit a future claim for shortages."

"Charlie thinks claims damage our customer relations, Jack."

"They do if they are unreasonable, but in your case a claim for shortages would definitely be reasonable, had you given the Consortium notice of it."

"I see what you mean."

"All right. Now, regarding the big change order you're estimating at present, when will you be finished with it?"

"I should have it finalized sometime tomorrow morning."

"Are you allowing sufficient labor for it?"

"It's hard to determine the exact number of labor hours required for the work, but I intend to double them, to be on the safe side."

"Okay, but let me have a look at the estimate before you submit it."

Just before noon next day, Jack studied Joe's estimate for the instrument relocation work. The estimate was certainly liberal, but with this type of work—difficulties anticipated with the relocation of existing work, no one could be certain about the time required for it. Jack called Joe again to join him in the boardroom.

"Joe, I've looked over your labor estimate, and I'm advising you to triple it."

"What? You can't be serious, Jack. I have already allowed more labor than a normal installation would take. Frank Butler will never approve any additional amount."

"I think he will, Joe. Just go ahead and triple the labor you've allowed in your estimate and then submit it."

"Okay, but I hope you know what you're doing, Jack."

"I know exactly what I'm doing," thought Jack, "I'm trying to recover some of your division's losses on the extra work you've done on this project. I'm gambling that Frank Butler has no time left to argue about the cost and that he doesn't know anything about instrumentation and what is involved to relocate instruments."

Charles Bourdain came to see Jack just before quitting time. "How's your investigation coming, Jack?"

"I think I have all I need."

"Will you be heading back, then?"

"Yes, tomorrow morning."

"Can I treat you for dinner at the Harvest Room in the MacDonald Hotel?"

"That'll be fine, Charlie." Jack knew that Charlie was anxious to find out what he would report to Harry.

As they relaxed over a cup of coffee and a brandy after dinner that evening Charles said, "Do you mind telling me what your investigation revealed, Jack?"

"Not at all. I think the company would be better off if you used MDF's system of estimating extra work. MDF is including more cost items. Furthermore, I think you should object in writing to any cutbacks by the owners of your estimated cost. That way you can submit a future claim if you can prove that the cutbacks caused you a damage."

"I don't mind switching to MDF's system, Jack, but I have some reservations regarding a possible claim."

"I know. Joe told me about your reservation. However, without written objections to the Consortium's cutbacks you have no way to recover anything, which is what you should be doing now to offset your losses."

"I'll have to give that some more thought, Jack. Anything else?"

"Yes. You might as well know that I've instructed Joe to triple his estimate for relocating the instruments."

"Is that wise? I mean, Frank Butler may object and just issue another cutback."

"I don't think he has time to argue about the cost, Charlie. He's in a pickle to get the upgrader project commissioned. Besides, we need to recover some of the losses he dealt us on the previous extra work orders."

"I know what you're trying to accomplish, Jack. I'm just unsure if it will work."

"We'll know soon enough, Charlie."

Back in Toronto Jack reported his findings to Harry. Two days later, Charlie informed Jack that Frank Butler had approved their estimate for the instrument relocation and issued the extra work order.

13

The following week Harry called Jack and asked him to investigate and assess a construction company in Whitehorse, Yukon for possible acquisition by MDF. He explained that acquiring a local, well-run company made more sense than opening a brand new branch with MDF staff.

"Your contact is a chap named Ben Hendricks, the owner of Polar Construction," Harry said. "Fiona will give you a brief history and the latest financial statement of the company, but you'll have to fly to Whitehorse to take a closer look at their assets and operation. Ben Hendricks is expecting you. He wants a million dollars for his company. I don't mind paying him a million dollars if I'm buying value, if you know what I mean. Let me have your report as soon as possible."

Two days later, Jack flew to Whitehorse and checked into the Best Western Gold Rush Inn on Main Street. He phoned Ben Hendricks at home to make an appointment. Mr. Hendricks promised to pick Jack up at his hotel in the morning and take him to a few of Polar's construction sites.

They visited two construction sites before noon and stopped for lunch at a small Klondike café. Ben Hendricks promised Jack the best BCT omelet Whitehorse had to offer.

"BCT?" Jack asked.

"Yes—bacon, celery, and tomato," said Ben. They were conversing on a first-name basis by then.

"I look forward to that," said Jack.

"You made a few notes at the jobsites," said Ben. "May I ask what interested you?"

"Sure. For one thing, I noticed that you stockpiled numerous construction materials. Do the owners allow you to bill for them before they are installed?"

"It depends on the owners. On the first jobsite they don't allow it and the stock stays in our inventory. On the second jobsite they allow it, but we have to bill it separately, and the billing for delivered materials cannot exceed fifty percent of the remaining billing for construction completion—if it does the owners deduct it from the construction completion billing. In this way, the delivered material billings disappear completely at the final construction completion billing."

"Very interesting," said Jack.

"On the next jobsite, which we'll visit after lunch, the owners only pay for delivered materials if these materials are stored in a bonded warehouse or fenced-in yard, which adds to our transportation cost. May I ask why you're so interested in this aspect?"

"Sure. I also made notes regarding my estimate of construction completion, which I'll check later against your billing totals. Stockpiled materials could affect the completion percentages, unless the billings are separated."

"I see now why Harry Broughton sent you to assess my company and operation, Jack."

Jack laughed. "It's just routine, Ben," he assured him. "I have to make sure that the projects can be completed with the money remaining to be billed to the customers."

Ben gave him an appraising look, then roared with laughter and said, "Let's enjoy that BCT omelet, shall we?"

After lunch they visited the third construction site and ended up at Ben's office building. Ben introduced Jack to his wife, Irene, who was the company's official bookkeeper, and led him into his office. The office looked more like a living room than an office and they sat down in easy chairs around a rough-hewn coffee table. The décor was definitely Yukon stylish, with stuffed heads of elk, moose, and polar bears.

Ben produced a bottle of brandy and a pitcher of water, and offered Jack a drink. Jack thanked him, and asked, "Who owns this building, Ben?"

"Polar Construction."

"What about the construction equipment—cranes, bulldozers, etcetera?"

"Also Polar Construction. Why do you ask?"

"At MDF we rent real estate and major construction equipment. It improves our financial ratios. That's what the banks and bonding companies like, Ben."

"I see," said Ben. "Perhaps my desire to own things is working against me, eh?"

Jack shrugged his shoulders. "You might consider selling the buildings and equipment to yourself, and then renting them back to the company, Ben. That way, you fulfill your desire to own things, and the company benefits financially."

"By gosh, Jack, I've never thought of it like that."

Jack explained to Ben how his company's financial ratios would improve with such a move. Then he said, "I'll need your last five years' financial statements as well, Ben."

"I'll get Irene to run off some copies for you. Do you think you'll have time to join us for supper tonight, Jack? Irene makes some of the best venison stew in Whitehorse."

Jack accepted the invitation, and got up to leave. He waited for Irene to make him the copies of the financial statements and Ben drove him back to the hotel, offering to pick him up at seven thirty. Jack said he would prefer a walk and Ben handed him a slip with their home address.

Back in his room Jack took a shower, dressed for the evening, and went to the hotel lounge to relax with a drink. He took a gander at the balance sheets of the financial statements. As he had suspected, fixed assets and inventories prevailed. With a few asset sales, the company could expand enormously. He made a mental note to check the values of both.

The evening with the Hendricks was enjoyable. Irene served her venison stew and Ben served his homemade wine. The northern country décor of their home added to Jack's comfort and relaxation. After supper Ben told some whopping fishing and hunting stories and Jack was sad to leave at midnight. He arranged for Ben to pick him up for lunch next day.

Jack spent the next morning going over the financial statements with a fine-toothed comb, checking some real estate values and determining Polar Construction's main competitors. He was ready when Ben picked him up at eleven thirty.

Ben took Jack to his local club for lunch. They ordered bear paw, the house specialty, and a Merlot wine to supplement it. While they were waiting for their meals Ben asked, "Did you spend a rewarding morning?"

Jack said, "I went over your financial statements, and aside from the excessive fixed assets, your balance sheet looks okay, providing the inventory amount can be justified. Your yearly growth is barely six percent—nothing to brag about, but you can improve it with the sale of fixed assets, which increases your bonding capacity. Your cash flow looks okay, but I want to have a closer look at it. Cash flows can be manipulated—inadvertently sometimes," he added quickly when he saw the shadow on Ben's face.

"Excuse my ignorance, Jack, but just how would you manipulate cash flows?"

"The easiest way is to move billings from one fiscal period to another, and contractors are famous for generating cash flows by overbilling their work. Another way is to over- or understate your inventory."

"How would you do that? Isn't inventory usually based on what it cost?"

"Yes, but inventory can get outdated or it can appreciate in value over time, and that is the excuse executives use for manipulating the values of their inventory."

"Well, I'll be damned—I learn something new every day. However, I think you'll find my cash flows quite legitimate, Jack."

"I hope so, Ben, because Harry Broughton would be very unhappy if it were otherwise. I'll know more after I analyze your operational statements. Incidentally, the bear paw is excellent."

Jack spent the afternoon analyzing the Polar Construction operational statements. He was satisfied that most entries were legitimate but he noticed that the administrative salary entries were rather low. He phoned Ben to enquire about the reason for this. Ben told him that upon the advice of their accountant he and his wife did not draw a salary but paid themselves a dividend. Jack enquired who else was receiving dividends. Ben told him that the company is family owned. He held fifty percent of the shares, his wife thirty percent, and their two children ten percent each. Jack thanked him and continued with his calculations.

After a while Jack looked up with a heavy sigh. He liked Ben, but he had no doubt in his mind that Ben had used one of the oldest tricks to manipulate his cash flow. Perhaps he did it inadvertently or perhaps upon the advice of his accountant, but he had done it nevertheless. The dividend paid by the company may be sufficient as a salary for his wife, in her position as bookkeeper, but it was far too little for Ben as the manager and CEO of a construction company. Jack estimated that Ben shortchanged himself by at least $150,000 a year. This would take care of most of the cash flow, which would leave the company barely profitable.

Jack noted that until two years back, their dividend was much larger. He assumed that they cut it on advice of their accountant, who may have tried to improve the financial statements in anticipation of a sale of the company. He knew that Harry would never buy into it.

Jack called Ben and said, "I'm flying back to Toronto in the morning, Ben, and I'd like to reciprocate your hospitality by inviting you and your wife out for dinner tonight."

"It's Irene's bridge night tonight, but I'm honored to accept your invitation, Jack."

After they finished their elk steaks and half a bottle of wine, Ben asked, "Are you at liberty to divulge your report to Harry Broughton about Polar Construction, Jack?"

"I don't think Harry would object. I have already told you about your excessive fixed asset position, but you can fix that, and I'm taking your inventory figures at face value. However, I'm concerned about your cash flow, Ben."

"But Harry Broughton himself told me that he was impressed with my cash flow, Jack."

Jack shrugged. "Harry didn't know that your only salary consisted of a meager dividend, Ben—far too little for a construction company manager and CEO. If MDF buys your company, it would have to pay someone in your position at least another $150,000 a year—there goes most of your cash flow."

Ben looked at Jack admiringly. "I hope Harry Broughton pays you well," he said. "If not, come and see me."

Jack smiled and got up. He held out his hand and said, "Thanks, Ben. It's been a pleasure meeting you and Irene."

Back in Toronto, Jack gave Harry his report. Harry looked disappointed. Jack said, "You could establish a more profitable division up there for half a million dollars."

"I know, but I don't like the start-up risks."

Jack looked surprised. He had never heard Harry complain about risks. Harry saw Jack's surprised look and added, "The problem is that I don't have much time to devote to another division, Jack."

Now he really had Jack puzzled. Harry had enough capable staff members to accomplish this.

Harry asked, "Did you have a chance to check on the construction activity up there?"

"I did. There seems to be enough commercial construction, but I didn't notice much industrial work. Don't look so glum about losing Polar Construction, Harry. Aside from their fixed assets and inventory, the company isn't worth much."

"You're right, of course. Let's forget about it."

14

A few days after Mary had transferred to MDF's Toronto office. Knowing her love for seafood, Jack invited her to a sumptuous dinner at his favorite seafood restaurant for Friday evening.

Jack looked closely at Mary while she was deciding what to order. He liked the natural color of her skin, devoid of makeup. Her shining brown hair framed her beautiful, oval face admirably. For jewelry she wore small, golden pendant earrings and a thin, golden necklace with a matching pendant. She had long fingers, the fingers of an artist, with natural nail polish to preserve the moisture and make them more pliable. The colors of her clinging beige dress, with a neatly balanced, unobtrusive, blue design, nicely set off the curves of her figure. No doubt in his mind, this woman had class.

She looked up at him from her menu and asked, "Have you ever tried the Chilean sea bass, Jack?"

"I sure have," he replied. "It beats everything else on the menu."

"I think I'll order it, then. You must really like seafood, Jack."

"No, not particularly, I like it when it's well prepared. I also like Chinese, Japanese, and Korean foods—and Greek and Italian foods, for that matter."

"I love Asian dishes, too, and Italian ones, but I've not had any Greek dishes, except for Greek salads."

"Well, I'll have to introduce you to my favorite Greek restaurant, then, won't I?"

She laughed. "I'll look forward to it. Do Greeks offer seafood dishes?"

"They do. Most nationalities have certain seafoods as one of their specialties. The Danes love smoked eel, the Norwegians love herring, the Swedes love sardines, and so on. I eat more seafood when I visit islands. The seafood seems fresher and tastier, somehow."

"Which islands do you visit, Jack?"

"Oh, I go mostly to the Caribbean and the Bermuda Islands."

"I learned to love seafood dishes on the Hawaiian Islands," said Mary.

"I've never been there."

"They are very beautiful, very romantic. I'm sure you'd love it there, Jack."

"I've heard that they are too commercialized."

"Oahu, perhaps, but the other islands still maintain some of their pristine origin. What do you do on your visits to the islands, Jack?"

"I go sightseeing, of course, and search for good restaurants, but mostly I relax on the beaches, letting the surf sounds flow over me, reading good books by my favorite authors."

"And who are your favorite authors, if I may ask?"

"I like Len Deighton for his spy novels, and John le Carré, of course. I like Colin Dexter for his detective novels, and Wilbur Smith for his adventure novels, and I like W. Somerset Maugham's stories. I like Michael Palin for his travelogues. I like Bertrand Russell for his philosophical views, and I like Henry Miller for his honest autobiographies. I also like Edward de Bono for his instructions on how to think outside the box. These are just a few authors whose books I may take with me on my travels, Mary."

"I have read books by all of these authors, except Edward de Bono."

"Edward de Bono is a teacher. He teaches interesting methods of thought directions. I think you would enjoy his books. I can lend you mine, if you like."

"I would appreciate that."

"I'm also interested in the music and paintings of the islanders, Mary."

"So am I. The Hawaiian melodies are very moving and romantic, and Hawaiian paintings preserve their pristine spirits, I believe. Are you a music lover, too, Jack?"

"I love the old-time dance music—tangos, waltzes, and so on."

"So do I. You must take me dancing sometime, to a band that specializes in these dances."

"I look forward to it. I especially like tangos and waltzes. Which are your favorite dances?"

"I love tangos and waltzes, but I also like sambas, and rumbas."

"I can't wait to dance these dances with you, Mary."

She laughed and gave him an enticing look.

After they had finished their main course he enquired if she would like some dessert. She declined and he suggested a nightcap at his downtown apartment.

When they entered his place, she was astonished at the size of it and admired his smart décor, especially his well-chosen paintings. "These paintings are very different," she said. "Where did you get them?"

"Oh, I picked them up during my travels mostly. Do you like them?"

"Like them? I love them! They are beautiful, and they complement the marine décor. I also love your teak furniture. It makes me feel like I'm traveling on a luxury liner."

As he poured their Kahlúa drinks, she looked critically at a picture of a gracious looking woman and asked, "Who's your admiration?"

"My mother," he answered her. "She is a wonderful woman."

"Does she live here in Toronto?"

"No, she retired to Boca Raton in Florida after my father died."

"I like her kind facial expression," Mary said admiringly.

"She is very kind."

They sat down on the living room sofa and soon started necking. After they enjoyed their Kahlúa drinks and a passionate kiss Jack said, "I'll introduce you to my bedroom."

She admired the bedroom as much as the living room and told him he had good taste. They looked at each other longingly for a moment, then stripped naked, went to bed, continued their passionate kiss, and enjoyed each other's body until they climaxed together. Exhausted, they stayed for another half hour, coupled in an embrace.

Then Mary kissed him gently and whispered, "I have to go to the bathroom."

Waiting for her to return, Jack reflected on their recent ecstasy until he grew hard again. When she came back and noticed his erection, she immediately fell in love with it, took it in her hands, and placed a lingering kiss on it. He quickly reached another climax. Groaning with gratification, he turned around and reciprocated. Mary got so aroused that she screamed with pleasure as she convulsed with her own intense climax.

In the morning Jack made some toast and coffee and fried some bacon and eggs. The alluring smell awoke Mary and she rushed to the bathroom for a quick shower.

Compatible in so many ways, they decided, over breakfast, to start living together. Jack offered his spacious apartment as their common abode and Mary accepted his offer with enthusiasm. Both were happy beyond words.

Jack and Mary spent the rest of the day picking up Mary's clothing and purchasing a few personal things to replace the ones she had left behind when leaving Calgary. They also bought enough groceries for at least a week and Mary offered to cook them an Italian dinner. Jack told Mary his favorite dish was macaroni and tomato sauce with meatballs. She laughed and said, "Consider it done. Nothing could be simpler."

After dinner Mary frowned and said, "I wonder if Harry will object to our living arrangement. I'll have to tell Fiona. She helped me find my apartment in Toronto."

"I doubt that Harry will be concerned about our living arrangement. If anything, he may think about possible conflicts of interest, but I don't think he'll be too concerned about that either. Relax, Mary. How about going to see a movie tonight?"

She smiled. "I bet you have one in mind already."

"Yes, I do. Today's newspaper advertises a Russian submarine movie that looks interesting. Would you like to see it?"

"I'd love to see it. I'm interested in all kinds of adventure movies."

They finished the weekend taking a drive into the country.

15

Jack met Harry for lunch on Monday. Harry said, "I hear via the grapevine that Mary moved in with you."

Jack thought, Mary must have told Fiona this morning—so much for trusting Fiona with anything. Her first loyalty was to Harry, especially if potential conflicts of interest within the company may be involved.

"You've heard correctly," he said.

Harry gave him an appraising look. "Anytime you two decide to get married, let me know. I'd like to be part of it."

"You'll be the first to know, Harry," Jack replied.

"Good. Now let's talk some business. Our Manitoba Division Manager, David Conserat, seems to have run into a major delay on a research laboratory. The building owners have already been in touch with me with threatening remarks. I promised them to send my Customer Relations VP to investigate and resolve the matter."

"What caused the delay, Harry?"

"It's a long and complex story, but I'll give you the gist of it. David placed a purchase order with a Winnipeg wholesaler for a large transformer that supplies the power to the building. The trucker ran into a detour, toppled, and damaged the transformer. The wholesaler ordered the trucking company to return the transformer to the manufacturer for repair. The manufacturers refuse to repair the transformer until they receive payment, not only for the transformer but also for the repair of it. David refuses to pay for it until he receives it, and the wholesaler cannot pay for it until he receives payment from MDF. It's a mess. There are more legal aspects involved, but that's the gist of it. We have to find a solution immediately to avoid a major delay claim against us by the building owners. The owners are nearly finished furnishing and staffing the building."

Jack said, "I better leave for Winnipeg this afternoon."

"That's my recommendation, Jack. You have full authority to take any action necessary to satisfy our customer, the building owners. And remember—time is of the essence."

Jack drove home, packed a carry-on, wrote a quick note for Mary, and left for the airport. He checked into the Fairmont Winnipeg Hotel at eight and phoned David Conserat at home.

David answered on the first ring. "Hello Jack, welcome to Winnipeg. Harry phoned me this afternoon to let me know you're coming. What's your plan?"

"Meet me at seven for breakfast, David, and we'll go from there. I'm staying at the Fairmont."

David Conserat was a stocky fellow, of medium height, with a receding hairline, and a mustache. He arrived at the hotel coffee shop promptly at seven, and greeted Jack warmly. After he placed his bacon and eggs order Jack asked him, "How did you get involved in a transformer purchase, David?"

"The electrical subcontractor we chose for this project has limited credit available, so we agreed to purchase the transformer for him."

"Can you give me the details of the purchase order?"

"Sure: The transformer description followed the engineer's specifications—we requested a firm delivery date, and delivery terms free on board the research building, as per our standard procedure, Jack."

"Then how come the manufacturer wants payment for non-delivery of the transformer?"

"Because, unbeknownst to us, the wholesaler placed his order with the manufacturer free on board factory, at the manufacturer's inflexible insistence."

Jack whistled and was quiet for a while, knowing the situation triggered an interesting legal problem. "Did the wholesaler hire the trucking company?" he wanted to know.

"Yes, and that adds to the problem. The primary trucking company with whom the wholesaler has the contract hired a secondary trucking company because they don't truck farther west than Toronto, and the secondary trucking company ran into a roadblock and detour on the way to Winnipeg. They blame the poor condition of the detour road for the accident and involved the Province of Ontario in a claim for damages."

"Good luck," said Jack. "What's our law firm's position?"

"They have already issued a statement of claim against the wholesaler."

"How is that going to get the project completed?"

David shrugged his shoulders. "That's where you come in, I guess."

"I better have a meeting with them. What are you doing to give the owners temporary power, David?"

"The only transformers we could find in a hurry are owned by the City of Winnipeg—much smaller than what we need, but they can use several of them to build a bank. Their transformers are outdoor types and we have to build a fenced-in concrete pad for them. The City will do the transformer installation and primary connections, for a prohibitive price, of course, and our electrical subcontractor will do the temporary secondary connections."

Jack nodded. This would get them by until the owners required more power. "Anything else?"

"Yes. We left an opening to receive the contract transformer, which we have to temporarily hoard."

"I'd like to take a look at the building, David. Then I'll meet with our legal counsel after lunch."

"Sure thing, Jack. I'll take you to the site."

The owners' activity at the site surprised Jack. He understood now why Harry was concerned. However, he was satisfied that David had taken the appropriate action, so far. After their jobsite visit, Jack and David stopped for lunch and then proceeded to their Winnipeg law firm's offices.

The lawyer handling the case, Bill Hassel, was a tall, dark-haired, lean-faced individual with keen, blue eyes. "How can I help you, gentlemen?" he wanted to know.

"We're concerned that taking the legal route is not going to satisfy our customer, who is badly in need of power," Jack replied.

"That is your concern," he shot back. "My concern is to protect your legal position."

"Yes, but our legal position with the building owners must also be protected," Jack countered.

"Your contract with the owners is protected by a *force majeure* clause. If they want to sue for delays, we'll face that when the time comes."

"That will do nothing to maintain our customer relations, Mr. Hassel."

He shrugged. "I'm here to protect your legal rights. If you want anything else, you'll have to hire a public relations expert."

Jack got up and held out his hand. "Well thanks for seeing us on such short notice, Mr. Hassel."

"Don't mention it."

Jack decided to have a brief meeting with the building owners' representative the next morning to apprise them of what MDF was doing to provide them a measure of power. Then he flew to Montreal to meet with the manufacturer.

He checked into The Queen Elizabeth Hotel later that day and made an appointment to meet with the transformer's factory manager, Ian MacDonald, in the morning.

The transformer factory was located on the outskirts of Montreal. Ian MacDonald took Jack first to the factory floor to look at the damages caused to the transformer. Then he took him into a meeting room. He explained that, fortunately, they had drained the oil from the transformer to meet Environment Canada's regulation for hazardous materials. Otherwise, the severe damage to the cooling fins would have caused leakage and an environmental cleanup situation. He said that they fill the transformer for testing purposes and then remove the oil and ship it separately.

Jack asked, "What will it cost to repair the damage and retest the transformer?"

"Our cost would run in the neighborhood of twelve thousand."

"How long would it take you to do the job?"

"About ten days for the damage and four days for the testing."

"Would you consider selling the transformer to MDF, Mr. MacDonald?"

"We normally go through wholesalers, for obvious reasons, but we could consider selling directly to the consumer in these circumstances. The wholesaler has flatly refused to pay for it, you know."

"MDF would like to give you a purchase order to cover the price of the transformer and the cost of repairing and retesting it. Would that be acceptable to you?"

"We would require payment in advance, Mr. Malone. I hope you understand our position."

"I do. Can we agree on a fixed price?"

Ian MacDonald mentioned a figure that was well below MDF's purchase order price with the wholesaler. However, when Jack mentally added estimates for the shipping and temporary transformer bank costs, MDF would nearly break even.

Jack got up and held out his hand. "You've got yourself a deal, Mr. MacDonald. Let me have your banking information and I'll arrange for a money transfer to your account today. Can we agree on a pick-up date fifteen days from today?"

"You can rely on it, Mr. Malone."

"Okay. I'll also send you a purchase order, for the record."

On the way back to his hotel Jack stopped at the CN Railway office to make shipping arrangements for the transformer. He issued instructions for the transformer pick-up at the factory in fifteen days, the transportation by rail to Winnipeg, and the delivery to the research building. He asked for an estimated delivery time. The official promised him ten days from time of pick-up. Jack was satisfied.

From his hotel room, he phoned David for instructions on where to make the money transfer, what to put in the purchase orders for the transformer and its transport, and to write a registered letter to the wholesaler canceling MDF's purchase order for the transformer because of failure to deliver as ordered.

Next, he phoned Bill Hassel and informed him of his actions. "I don't like it," said Bill. "You're inviting a lawsuit from the wholesaler for loss of profit."

"I leave such details to you, Mr. Hassel. After all, you're our legal expert. I'm just interested in keeping our customer happy."

Last, Jack phoned the building owners' representative in Winnipeg and apprised him of his actions to get the transformer repaired and delivered to site. He added, "I'm sure the installation will be completed in less than two months."

"If you can accomplish that, Mr. Malone, I can guarantee you that we won't have a claim against MDF."

Jack smiled. No use telling the representative that a claim would not have been legally collectible. That would just harm their customer relations.

That evening, Jack treated himself to a well-earned dinner, with a bottle of Châteauneuf-du-Pape. He also phoned Mary and asked her how she would like to spend a week in Victoria with him.

Jack reported to Harry just before noon on Friday. After Harry listened carefully to Jack, he said, "You did well, Jack. I couldn't have done it better. Regardless of what our lawyers tell us, let's never forget that the customer is always right."

"I'd like to take a week's vacation in Victoria, Harry."

"Okay, but stop in Vancouver and meet with Roger Hamilton regarding some problems he is having with a unit-price contract. And while you're there, find out why the engineers of the oil upgrader reject instruments that they specified by catalogue number."

16

Jack checked into the Fairmont Waterfront Hotel in Vancouver and phoned Roger Hamilton, MDF's Western Division Manager. They agreed to meet for dinner at the Five Sails Restaurant. Roger didn't mind spending an evening with Jack. After all, Jack made a special stopover in Vancouver to see him. Roger was a medium-built, brown-haired, brown-eyed man in his late forties.

"Beautiful view of the bay from here," said Jack.

"Yes. This restaurant is renowned not only for its view but also for its food," replied Roger.

"Harry tells me that you have a unit-price contract that could spell trouble."

"It has already spelled trouble," said Roger. "The owners of a huge loading facility up at Prince Rupert decided to divide the work between three contractors. Even though the contractors submitted a tender of their unit prices for the work, the owners made sure these unit prices weren't too far apart. It's what's known as constructive negotiations between the contractors and the owners."

"But I gather that is not what's causing the trouble," said Jack.

"No. What's causing the trouble is disruptive interference between the contractors."

"Can you be more specific, Roger?"

"Well, we maintain a crew up there to do our contract work, and if the crew cannot proceed because of some work the other contractor must do first we run into stand-by time that is not included in our unit prices."

"I see. Did you really need this type of work, Roger? It seems a nuisance to me, even without any disruptions."

"You're right. I wish I'd never heard of the job. We were running low on work for a while and bid on anything that came along."

"Unit-price contracts can be useful in ways other than making a profit on them," said Jack.

"Can you explain that to me?"

"Well, keeping track of when the work is done for unit-price billing purposes should be expanded to keep track of the labor used for each unit price. Thus, you find out immediately when differences occur. Your labor units are either too high or they are too low, in which case you can adjust them. Sometimes another influence causes the difference, which you must immediately investigate. Other influences could be internal—caused by your own crews—or external. If internal, you can take timely remedial action, and if external, you can give timely notice to the party causing the problem for a claim against any experienced losses. That is the useful part of unit-price contracts. In a lump-sum contract, you usually find out too late what's going on, if you find out at all."

"I see what you mean. It's similar to the work assessment method for each construction area."

"Exactly.

"In our case, the lost time we're experiencing can easily be traced to other contractors on site whose work must precede ours. We based our unit prices on uninterrupted construction progress. Can we be faulted for that?"

"I don't believe you can be faulted for that, Roger. One clause in the specifications Harry gave me says 'the owners' representative shall coordinate the work of all contractors on site.' To me, that means the owners' rep must make sure that all the work proceeds without disruptions."

"We pointed that out to the owners' rep, Jack, but he interprets the clause differently. He says it is his job to make sure that when Task A is completed the work of Task B follows immediately. He says he cannot be held responsible if the crews for Task B experienced stand-by time waiting for Task A to be completed."

"Hmm. I think he has a point, Roger. Normally, when we are in control of all construction work on site, we try to keep stand-by time to a minimum, but when several contractors are involved, stand-by time becomes more of an issue. What, if anything, did you allow for stand-by time in your unit prices?"

"Nothing, Jack. We analyzed the work involved for each unit price and allowed only the bare minimum. You know how it is when you're up against tough competition. We didn't expect to have to wait for other contractors to do their jobs and hold us up if they run into trouble."

"I suppose you did not submit a unit price for stand-by time," Jack smiled. "I'm just joking, Roger. I'll talk to the owners' rep and see if a solution to the problem can be found."

"Be my guest, Jack. You'll find him extremely hard-nosed."

"One other thing, Roger. What is the issue with the rejected instruments at the oil upgrader?"

"The engineers claim that the instruments don't meet their performance specifications and that MDF must replace them with proper instruments. The engineers are withholding a substantial amount of contract money to cover the so-called deficiency."

"What's your position, Roger?"

"My position is that we ordered the instruments by the engineers' specified catalogue number and we're refusing to replace them without a change order. Harry phoned me and said you'll get involved in the dispute, so I brought along the relevant specification pages for you." He handed Jack two folded pages.

"Who's the engineer you're dealing with?"

"A chap named Dick Strong."

"Okay. I'll take a look at the specs and give him a call tomorrow."

"Thanks, Jack."

The following morning Jack phoned the owners' loading facility rep, a chap by the name of Ralph Werner. A gruff, deep voice answered after the first ring.

"Prince Rupert Loading Facility."

"Mr. Werner, please."

"Speaking. Who wants him?"

"Jack Malone, VP Customer Relations from MDF. I'd like to discuss with you how we can eliminate some of the stand-by time we're experiencing on your jobsite, Mr. Werner."

"I have already discussed this with your project manager."

"I'm aware of that, but I'm also interested in finding a solution—with your help, of course."

"Well, there's not much I can do about it. MDF should have incorporated stand-by time in its unit prices."

"MDF tried to give you the lowest possible unit prices anticipating no stand-by time, Mr. Werner. They did not count on other contractors' problems holding them up."

Ralph Werner was silent for a few seconds. Jack asked, "Are you still there?"

"I'm still here. I'm just trying to think of something. I can let your crews have some cost-plus work, I suppose, which I'm contemplating, providing we can agree on a reasonable labor rate and material markup."

"I'm sure Roger Hamilton, our Western Division Manager, can work out satisfactory rates for you, Mr. Werner."

"Okay. Tell him to contact me and I'll see what I can do for you guys."

"Thank you very much."

"Don't mention it. Just make sure MDF doesn't hold up any contractors."

Why the sudden change of heart? Jack was wondering.

Jack had an appointment to see Dick Strong right after lunch. Dick Strong met him in the lobby of the engineering office. He was a tall, broad-shouldered individual with a ruddy face and graying hair.

"How do you do, Mr. Malone? Please follow me to the boardroom."

A secretary brought them a pot of hot coffee and cups.

"What can I do for you, Mr. Malone?" asked Dick Strong.

"I'm here to discuss the instrument rejection with you, Mr. Strong."

"The rejection seems straightforward, Mr. Malone. They don't meet our performance requirements."

"I had a look at the specifications, Mr. Strong. The specifications merely mention that the instruments measure the oil flow and give us a catalogue number, or approved equal. MDF ordered the specified catalogue number."

"Besides measuring the oil flow, Mr. Malone, the measurement must also meet an acceptable tolerance level of accuracy and your instruments do not accomplish this."

"The specifications do not mention an acceptable level of tolerance, Mr. Strong."

"That should be automatic, Mr. Malone. MDF is experienced in this type of construction."

"Nevertheless, you gave us a catalogue number to use and we used it. If the catalogue number does not meet your required tolerance level, it is not our concern, but yours."

"The instruments are designed to measure light oil flows with acceptable accuracy, but heavy oil flows introduce an unacceptable inaccuracy, Mr. Malone."

"I can appreciate that, Mr. Strong, but the specifications do not mention a required level of accuracy. The flow readings will just have to be adjusted by the inaccuracy factor."

"The owners will never accept this as a solution, Mr. Malone."

"Then you must find a better one, Mr. Strong."

"Yes, Mr. Malone, MDF must replace the instruments with the proper ones."

"We're quite willing to do this if you give us a written change order with your new requirements."

"The owners would simply refuse to pay for such a change order, Mr. Malone."

"Then you must find somebody else to pay for it, Mr. Strong."

"Do I take it that MDF is refusing to change the instruments free of charge?"

"Correct."

"What is the charge for changing the instruments?"

"The manufacturer wants forty percent of the purchase price to refurbish and restore the instruments and MDF requires eight hours for each instrument to remove it, package and ship it back, and reinstall the replacement."

Dick Strong looked at Jack silently for a couple of minutes. "Eight hours seems high," he said lamely.

"It's only an estimate. If it takes less time, we'll charge less. How's that?"

"Okay," said Dick Strong after a while. "Go ahead and change the instruments."

"As I said before—only with a written change order, Mr. Strong, giving us specific instructions and agreeing to our charges."

Dick Strong looked at him again for a minute. Then he said, "Wait here. I'll have one prepared." With that comment, he stormed out of the boardroom.

Jack took the chance to sip his cooled coffee.

Dick Strong returned after fifteen minutes with a typed up change order, which he plunked down in front of Jack.

Jack looked at it for a minute, and said, "I want it signed by you, and I want some time to check with the manufacturer to see if they can meet the specified accuracy level."

Dick Strong took the change order back and signed it, while commenting that time is of the essence.

Jack met Roger Hamilton again for dinner at the Five Sails. He told him about Ralph Werner's promise and gave him Dick Strong's change order.

Roger smiled appreciatively, and enquired, "How did you manage to get this change order out of Dick Strong, Jack?"

"Easy. The engineers forgot to mention the required accuracy of the instruments in their specs."

Roger laughed and shook his head. "I'm glad to have you on our side, Jack."

17

Jack called Harry from his hotel room and informed him of his actions regarding the unit-price contract and the rejected instruments. Harry was pleased but asked Jack to postpone his trip to Victoria.

"Something has come up in our Quebec Division, Jack, which I want you to investigate."

"Mind telling me what it is, Harry?"

"I'd like to discuss it with you personally."

"Okay, I'll head back to Toronto tomorrow."

"Fine. Call me when you get in."

After hanging up, Jack put a call through to Mary.

"How're you doing, Fantastic?"

"Fine, Lover Boy. I miss you, though."

"I miss you, too, but I'll see you sooner than I had expected. We'll have to postpone our Victoria vacation for a while. I'll be home tomorrow evening."

"I've looked forward to the trip, Jack, but seeing you again is all that counts. I'll prepare us your favorite Italian dish with some pork chops for dinner."

He laughed, "I was planning to take you out for dinner, Mary, but I like your offer better."

"See you tomorrow evening, then."

"Look forward to it, Fantastic!"

She gave him a sexy chuckle and said, "I'll make sure you won't be disappointed, Lover Boy."

Jack arrived at his Toronto office at eleven thirty and called Fiona to arrange a meeting with Harry. She told him that Harry was out but left a message for Jack to join him for lunch at the yacht club at one o'clock.

"He also left a manila folder with some reports for you to look at. I'll bring it to your office."

Jack had a quick look at the reports. They were progressive construction updates of a large laundry project in Montreal, signed by MDF's Quebec Division Manager Sylvain Boudreau. The earlier reports showed a six percent profit, which gradually disappeared in the later reports—down to one percent in the last report. This was nothing strange, as far as Jack was concerned. Profit is always the first item to disappear when things go wrong in construction. He put the file folder in his briefcase and left his office for the yacht club.

Harry was already enjoying a drink when Jack arrived. Jack ordered a vodka martini and enquired, "What did you want me to look at in Sylvain's reports, Harry?"

Harry waited for the waiter to leave and said, "I'm suspecting foul play, Jack. I have asked Sylvain some pertinent questions about his loss of profit and his answers don't satisfy me—not at all. He seems to be hiding something."

"Do you suspect foul play merely because of the disappeared profit, Harry? Profit always disappears as things go wrong."

"It's not just that, Jack. I made a site visit to the project a few weeks ago and the project manager was literally glowing with pride. He told me he had seldom managed a better project."

"There could be some estimating mistakes that the project manager is unaware of, Harry."

"It's possible, but I doubt it. In any case, I want you to investigate this problem."

"I think Sylvain will resent that."

"Then he should have given me more satisfying explanations."

"Well, I'll call Sylvain and tell him I'm coming in regard to a routine inspection, at your request. I'll fly to Montreal in the morning."

"Fine. Now let's enjoy the yacht club's sautéed pickerel special and a bottle of Chenin Blanc, Jack."

Back at the office Jack called Sylvain Boudreau. Brigit, his secretary answered.

"Is Sylvain in, Brigit?"

She recognized his voice and said, "Hang on a moment, Mr. Malone."

"What gives me the pleasure of your call, Jack?" Sylvain asked.

"I'll be in Montreal tomorrow, Sylvain. Are you free to join me for lunch?"

"No, but I can rearrange my schedule. Where are you staying?"

"At the Fairmont Queen Elizabeth. Let's have lunch in their dining room at eleven thirty."

"Okay. I'll see you tomorrow."

Jack finished his Vancouver reports for Harry, put Harry's Quebec report file in his briefcase, and left for home.

Mary got there ahead of him and greeted him with a deep kiss, snuggling close to him.

"Gosh, I've sure missed you, Lover Boy," she breathed heavily.

He felt a growing sensation in his groin and she must have felt it, too. "Be patient until after dinner," she said. "I have some fresh oysters for starters, and then your favorite Italian dish."

He smiled, gave her a peck on the cheek, and went to the bathroom. When he came out he asked her, "Why the oysters, Mary?"

"I read in one of the novels recently that they're a powerful aphrodisiac, Lover Boy."

"We'll confirm that later, I hope."

"Sure will!" she chuckled.

After Jack finished munching down his oysters Mary served Jack's favorite dish: macaroni noodles with her special creamy tomato sauce and meatballs. During dinner Mary asked him why they had to postpone their trip.

"Harry wants me to do a special investigation in Montreal. He's suspecting foul play in the Quebec Division."

"Is that an emergency?"

Jack laughed. "Anything that bothers Harry is an emergency, Mary, but don't worry, it won't take long. I just hope it's not going to end up in another firing."

"I hope you're not thinking of Sylvain Boudreau. He's such a nice man."

"I know, but if Harry is right about the foul play, Sylvain could get sacked. I wish I had never agreed to take this job, Mary."

"Why don't you just find yourself another job, Jack?"

"You mean quit MDF?"

"Yes, or ask Harry to reassign you to another position."

"Harry couldn't give me back my old division after appointing my second-in-command to my position."

"What about creating another division?"

"I suppose that's possible. A while back he was going to start one in the Yukon. But I'd hate to move to the Yukon, Mary."

"Me too. Couldn't you start your own business, like a management consulting firm?"

"I've thought of that, but it wouldn't solve my dilemma. I would still expose the shortcomings of employees and potentially get them fired."

"Well, let's think about it some more."

After they washed and dried the dishes they watched an African adventure movie for a couple of hours, and then decided to put Mary's aphrodisiac to the test. Jack was last to use the bathroom and when he returned Mary greeted him on the bed in a see-through negligee. Jack dropped his towel, exposing his ready erection, and joined her on the bed.

She gave him another passionate deep kiss that lingered, while Jack placed his right hand between her legs, enjoying the moisture of her sex, and said softly, "I sure love your moist readiness for love making, Fantastic."

For the next hour they enjoyed some passionate foreplay. Then, Jack whispered, "I can't hold it any longer, sweetheart."

She said, "I'm ready, too," and Jack entered her in the missionary position.

They continued their deep kiss, and, in seconds, each had an explosive orgasm. Jack still embraced her and kissed her gently for ten more minutes. Then, they went to the bathroom to shower together.

After they toweled each other dry Jack said, "I feel like continuing, Fantastic, but I have to get up early to catch a flight to Montreal."

Mary didn't object, but said, "Next time I'll find you a stronger aphrodisiac, Lover Boy, to remove any doubt about your priorities."

He laughed. "Look forward to it, Fantastic!"

18

Jack checked in at the Fairmont Queen Elizabeth at eleven, took his carry-on to his room, freshened up, and then went down to the dining room. Sylvain met him at the entrance and the maître d'hôtel showed them to their table.

They ordered cocktails and Sylvain asked, "What brings you to Montreal, Jack?"

"Harry is concerned about your laundry project and wants me to take a look at it," Jack replied.

"There's nothing to be concerned about," Sylvain shot back. "We didn't achieve our estimated profit, but that is nothing new. It happens all the time in this business. We encountered a few costly snags, that's all. I tried to explain that to Harry. It shouldn't concern him—we still made a small profit."

"Don't worry about it, then," Jack calmed him. "I'll just take a look at your records, perhaps make a site visit, then head back to Toronto, and, hopefully, assuage Harry's concerns."

"Well, it still bothers me, Jack. It's as if Harry doesn't trust me."

"Harry has a lot of money on the line, Sylvain. I suspect he just wants to cover his bases for the risks involved in construction, and profits are supposed to accomplish this. When profits disappear, his personal wealth is at stake. Every business manager knows that profits are required to cover risks. I shouldn't have to mention this to you, Sylvain."

"No use getting huffy with me, Jack. Of course I know that profits are required to cover risks, but Harry's mistrust still bothers me!"

"If he's out to lunch, in this case, Sylvain, I'll make sure to tell him. Let's forget about it and order some lunch."

They ordered steak sandwiches and a bottle of French Merlot. Their talk over lunch involved only trivial issues, and when they parted at two o'clock, Jack said, "I'll see you about nine tomorrow morning."

"Look forward to it, Jack." They shook hands and Jack went out for a walk.

The next morning when Jack arrived at Sylvain's office shortly after nine o'clock Brigit informed him that Sylvain had phoned her at eight thirty and requested that she convey his apologies to Jack for not meeting him as promised. She said he told her that he had given the matter he had discussed with Jack more thought last night and has decided to quit.

Jack was surprised, but didn't comment. He asked her, "Who is his second in command?"

"Marcel Charbonneau. He's out this morning."

"Okay, and who's your accountant?"

"Mrs. Gartner."

"Is there an office I can use?"

"How about the boardroom?"

"Fine. Please ask Mrs. Gartner to join me there for a few minutes."

She showed him to the boardroom and enquired, "Can I get you a cup of coffee, Mr. Malone?"

"Yes, a cup of black coffee would be welcome—no sugar, please."

He made himself comfortable in the boardroom and took some reports from his briefcase. When Mrs. Gartner arrived he told her to take a seat. She looked downhearted and he asked, "Is anything the matter, Mrs. Gartner?"

"I just heard about Mr. Boudreau's resignation," she answered him. "He was a wonderful man to work with, Mr. Malone."

"I'm sure he was," said Jack. "But business must carry on."

"Of course," she said sternly. "What can I do for you, Mr. Malone?"

"Please let me have your files for the laundry project's purchase orders and the major equipment suppliers' invoices. And by the way, do you have access to the project's estimate file?"

"No. Mr. Charbonneau has the estimate file."

A few minutes later, she brought him the files he had requested and asked, "Is there anything else I can do for you, Mr. Malone?"

"Not at the moment. Thanks, Mrs. Gartner. I'll let you know when I need more."

Jack busied himself looking at the purchase order and invoice files until noon. He detected no irregularities and packed up the files again. He stuffed his notes into his briefcase and on the way out he asked Brigit where he could find a good restaurant nearby. She directed him to a little French restaurant two blocks down the road.

"They serve an excellent duck confit," she said, "with *pommes de terre à la sarladaise* and braised red cabbage."

"Sounds appetizing. Would you care to join me?"

"Thanks, but I'm meeting a friend for lunch."

Jack enjoyed the duck confit with a glass of red wine. He wondered why Sylvain thought it necessary to quit. Was his pride hurt, or did he have something to hide? If the latter, he probably knew that it wouldn't take Jack long to detect it. Yet, Jack had not found anything noteworthy during his perusal of the purchase orders or the suppliers' invoices. Nevertheless, Jack still had to peruse the suppliers' quotations and MDF's estimate.

Back at the office Brigit told him that Marcel Charbonneau was in and Jack said, "Ask him to join me in the boardroom."

When Marcel came in, he shook hands with Jack and said, "I've heard a lot about you, Mr. Malone."

"Call me Jack, Marcel. I hope you've heard only good things."

"Not all good things, I'm afraid."

Jack gave him a searching look. If Sylvain was involved in foul play as Harry suspected, was Marcel part of it, or did he, perhaps, run across an irregularity he couldn't explain without exposing his boss?

Jack said, "Good is relative to one's viewpoint, Marcel."

"I suppose you're right. How can I help you?"

"I need to take a look at the estimate file for the laundry project, including the suppliers' quotations. Mrs. Gartner tells me it's in your care."

"I'll fetch it for you. Does this have anything to do with Sylvain's resignation?"

"I don't know why Sylvain resigned. He and I had a lunch together, yesterday, but he never mentioned that he intended to resign. What makes you think that the laundry estimate files might have something to do with his resignation?"

Marcel just shrugged. "I'll be back in a minute with the files for you, Jack."

Jack called Mrs. Gartner and requested the labor expenditure record for the laundry project. After Marcel returned with the estimate files, Jack compared the labor figures first. There were no noteworthy discrepancies. He spent the remainder of the afternoon comparing the estimate with the material expenditures. It did not surprise him to find major discrepancies in the purchases of the laundry equipment. However, the various quotes for the laundry equipment matched the estimate.

Jack decided to meet with the chosen equipment supplier. He put through a call, asked for the president, and was connected with a Mr. Richard Sabourin.

"My name is Jack Malone, Mr. Sabourin. I'm the Vice President of Customer Relations for MDF Industrial Constructors Inc. You're the supplier of the laundry equipment for our project in Montreal and I'd like to have a meeting with you. Would tomorrow suit you?"

"I am tied up in the morning until after lunch. Where are you staying, Mr. Malone?"

"At the Fairmont QE."

"Why don't I meet you at the Fairmont lounge for a drink at two o'clock, would that suit you?"

"Fine, Mr. Sabourin. I'll tell the waitress I'm expecting you and she'll show you to my table."

He bade the staff goodbye and left for the QE.

Jack spent the next morning shopping in the Old Town of Montreal. He found another French restaurant for lunch and then headed back to the Fairmont. He selected a quiet table in the lounge, gave the waitress his meeting instructions, ordered a vodka martini, and engrossed himself in The Globe and Mail.

Richard Sabourin arrived ten minutes late. "My apologies," he said, "traffic tie-up. It's not often we see people from MDF's head office, Mr. Malone. Does your visit have anything to do with Mr. Boudreau's departure?"

"I'm not sure why Mr. Boudreau departed, Mr. Sabourin. MDF's president, Harry Broughton, wanted me to investigate a concern he has with our cost over-runs at the laundry project. That is what I wanted to discuss with you today."

They waited until Mr. Sabourin received his drink and Jack added, "Most of your laundry equipment has been billed higher than what you have quoted us, Mr. Sabourin."

"But not higher than your purchase orders, Mr. Malone."

"True, but why the increase versus your quotes?"

"Mr. Boudreau wanted some controls prewired to save on-site labor."

"But that does not account for the enormous difference in cost, Mr. Sabourin."

Mr. Sabourin looked at Jack for a few seconds, then, said, "Mr. Boudreau also wanted some pay for services rendered, which we included in the price revision, Mr. Malone."

"Exactly what services rendered are we talking about?" Jack enquired.

Mr. Sabourin just stared at him.

Jack knew his question wouldn't be answered. Finally, he said, "Let me be blunt, Mr. Sabourin. We don't want to involve the RCMP, but we will if we have to. What we want is a credit for the so-called services rendered to you by Mr. Boudreau."

"But we have paid him!"

"That's your problem. Am I making myself clear, Mr. Sabourin?"

Mr. Sabourin got up without finishing his drink and said, "Yes, but I wish I had never met you, Mr. Malone."

"But can I report to my president that you will issue the credit, Mr. Sabourin?"

"Do I have a choice?"

"Frankly, no. When can we expect the credit?"

"Within a week. Goodbye, Mr. Malone. I hope to never see you again."

Jack checked out and made arrangements to fly back to Toronto. He also phoned Harry and assured him that his six percent profit on the laundry project would be reinstated within a week.

"How come?" Harry wanted to know.

"Overbilling by one of our suppliers," Jack said. "I'm on my way back to Toronto tonight. I will give you a full report tomorrow."

"Meet me for lunch at the yacht club, Jack."

"Okay."

When Jack gave Harry his report the following day Harry asked, "Should we take legal action against Sylvain?"

"I don't see an advantage in doing that, Harry. We'll get our money back, and anything else would just create an embarrassment to us."

"I suppose you're right, Jack. Okay, let's forget it. Thanks for clearing this issue up for me. I think I've lost some sleep over it."

Jack gave him a strange look. Surely Harry had not lost sleep over a reduced profit. What was his real concern? A nagging mistrust in one of his managers?

"Can I take my vacation now?" he asked.

"Of course, Jack. Sorry for the delay."

"Don't mention it, Harry."

19

Jack and Mary had a wonderful vacation in Victoria. They went whale watching, visited antique shops, found new restaurants every day, were overwhelmed by the beautiful flowers at the Butchart Gardens, and enjoyed their sexual exploits every night—and sometimes also in the morning, before breakfast.

One evening they were having a halibut dinner with a bottle of Chenin Blanc at Milestones. During their conversation Jack commented on the touchiness of Islamists when journalists mention the Islamists' Prophet Muhammad.

"They hold their prophet sacred, I guess," offered Mary. "By the way, what is your religion?"

"My parents were Baptists."

"Does that mean you're a Baptist?"

"No. To become a Baptist they must baptize you. I was never baptized. What about you, what's your religion?"

"My parents are Lutheran, and I was baptized as a baby, but I never developed a specific enthusiasm for any religion. If you're not a Baptist, Jack, do you have another religious belief?"

"I hate superstitions, but I do believe in Jesus Christ's philosophies—mainly love. Not only the physical love that we enjoy, but all types of love, including loving my enemies. Why are you so interested in my beliefs, Mary?"

She laughed. "I just want to make sure there are no religious hang-ups, in case you should ask me to marry you."

"Is that what you want, getting married I mean?"

"I like our relationship just as it is. I was just wondering if there were any hang-ups in case you should propose marriage."

"I see. However, I believe when two people love each other, marriage is redundant, unless they want to raise children."

She laughed. "I'm too old to want to raise any children, Jack."

"I'm getting a little old to raise children as well. By the way, I not only love your beautiful body, I also love your inner beauty. My love for you is all I need to make you my partner for life—till death us do part."

"Oh, Jack! Now look what you did." Tears were running down her cheeks. "I'm so happy," she sobbed. "I feel exactly the same love for you, Jack, and I am proud to be your partner for life."

He leaned over the table and gently kissed her tears away. "It's settled then," he assured her.

They spent two more days roaming Victoria and then returned to Toronto.

20

Jack sifted through his accumulated mail when Fiona came into his office unannounced.

"What did you do to Mary?" she asked. "She looks absolutely radiant."

Jack smiled. "I told her I love her, Fiona."

"You mean you love her beautiful body, don't you?"

"That, too, of course, but, no, I told her I love as a person—I love her inner beauty."

Fiona looked out of the window for a moment, deep in thought. Then, she said, "I was looking for a man all my adult life to tell me that."

"Be patient. You'll eventually find him. You're a very lovely woman, Fiona. I almost fell for you myself a few months ago, just after Harry offered me my new position."

She gave him an appraising look. "Why didn't you?" she wanted to know.

"I met Mary and fell in love with her."

She sadly looked out the window again. He thought he detected tears in her eyes. Then she turned around and said, "Did you ever come to grips with the concern you mentioned to me over our lunch?"

"You mean ratting on my friends?"

"Yes."

"Mary gave me a suggestion, which, I think, will resolve my dilemma."

"No wonder you're in love with her."

"She's a wonderful woman, Fiona."

Fiona nodded, lost in her own reverie for a while. Then she snapped out of it and said, "What I came to tell you, Jack, is that Harry wants to meet with you. He's out this morning but he said to meet him at the yacht club for lunch."

"Thanks, Fiona."

Jack arrived early at the yacht club. The club looked desolate now. Fall cleanup had already started, and the sail masts and the entire marina looked abandoned. He reflected again on the happy times he and Mary enjoyed in Victoria. They went for a vacation and came home joined for life. Love was truly a wonderful thing to behold.

Harry arrived close to one o'clock. "Sorry to be late," he said. "Have you ordered any food?"

"No. I was waiting for you."

"Fiona tells me you made Mary a happy woman."

"And she made me a happy man, Harry."

"Well, let's celebrate all that happiness."

Harry ordered a rare French brandy for them.

"The reason I want to meet with you is I received a joint-venture proposal from a Quebec company. They assure me that it could be mutually beneficial for all concerned. I have some doubts, and I want you to investigate the feasibility of the joint venture, Jack."

"What's the name of the Quebec company?"

"You may have heard of them—BJ Construction Consortium Inc."

"Yes, I've heard of them. They are mainly involved in construction management—very successful, from what I hear."

"BJCCI is partly owned by the Province of Quebec. They claim that as an advantage, but I have my doubts. They won't elaborate on this so-called advantage. That's why I want you to pay them a visit. They are headquartered in Montreal."

"Do you think they might tell me more than they have told you, Harry?"

"Probably not, but you have an intriguing way to get to the bottom of the issues involved. Besides, you should also talk to their competitors—get their views."

"Can you call BJCCI and line up an intro for my visit?"

"Certainly, that goes without saying. I'll let you have all the required contact information before you leave. Now, let's order some lunch. I'm starved."

Jack made a few more inquiries by phone regarding BJCCI and then left for Montreal two days later. He checked again into the Fairmont Queen Elizabeth.

Harry had already made an introduction on Jack's behalf with BJCCI's president, James Hill, and Jack called him to make an appointment for a meeting with him. "Where are you staying?" James Hill asked him.

"At the Fairmont QE."

"Are you free for lunch?"

"Yes."

"I could meet you at the QE at noon. They have an excellent dining room."

"That works for me, Mr. Hill."

Jack reserved a table in the dining room then went over his BJCCI notes once more. At noon he went down to the dining room and James Hill joined him a few minutes later. They ordered cocktails and James Hill asked, "What is the additional information you need, Mr. Malone—to what I had already given to Mr. Broughton?"

"Perhaps you can provide me with some details on the type of projects you have in mind for the joint ventures with MDF?"

"Certainly, Mr. Malone. The projects we have in mind would consist mostly of government-sponsored infrastructure, but we wouldn't have to be limited to those, if you know what I mean."

"I see—you're favoring government infrastructure because of the government's part ownership of your company, I presume?"

"That's correct. The government would give us first consideration regarding any construction tenders."

"How do your competitors feel regarding this preference you're receiving from the government?"

"This so-called preference is on the up-and-up, I can assure you, Mr. Malone."

"Can you explain that to me?"

"After the government closes bids, it determines if its budget is exceeded. If so, it asks the bidders to submit suggested savings—that's where we come in."

"Let me get this straight, Mr. Hill. You know the price of the lowest tender, and then submit a list of suggested savings that would not only beat the lowest tender but also provide additional savings to the government. Is that it?"

"Essentially, yes."

"And do your competitors ever end up with any government projects?"

"Of course, Mr. Malone, otherwise, they would stop bidding on them."

"I presume you would end up with the choicest projects, though?"

Mr. Hill smiled. "I think you've got the picture."

"Why do you need MDF at all under these favor-able circumstances, Mr. Hill?"

"Two reasons. One, MDF has more expertise and facilities for large projects of this nature. And, two, we at BJCCI require additional financing for these larger projects, which we believe MDF can provide."

"And what would BJCCI provide for these joint ventures, if I may ask?"

"We would make sure that any projects we desire would be approved by the government."

"Is that it? What about financial arrangements between MDF and BJCCI?"

"MDF would sign an agreement to pay BJCCI two percent of the contract price with the government, or fifty percent of the final profit on the project, whichever is greater."

"I see. And what happens if the project ends up incurring a loss, Mr. Hill?"

"The loss would not be shared by BJCCI, because MDF is solely in control of it."

"So, in summary, BJCCI puts up nothing but its influence with the government to land certain projects. MDF puts up the financing, the project management, the construction equipment, and half its profits, if any, otherwise two percent of the contract price. Is that it?"

"You've summed it up very well, Mr. Malone."

"Okay, I'll pass that on to Harry Broughton, and he'll get back to you."

The following day Jack met with Harry and gave him a complete report on his meeting with James Hill, and his own concern.

After some thought, Harry said, "Even if I liked the financial arrangements, Jack, which I don't, I like even less landing projects at our competitors' expense. That's not how MDF does business."

"I fully agree with you, Harry."

21

Jack called Harry. "Ted Stewart wants me to help him negotiate a claim settlement for the chemical plant near Edmonton, Harry." Ted Stewart was Brian Forbes' replacement at MDF's Alberta Division.

"He told me he had a solid claim," said Harry.

"Apparently, he has solid backup for the claim, but the owners' project manager is rejecting it."

"I see. How does he think you can help?"

"He thinks my position with MDF justifies me going over the owners' project manager's head."

"He has a point, but make sure he really has a solid claim, Jack."

After flying to Edmonton Jack checked into the Fairmont Hotel MacDonald just before noon and met Ted Stewart in The Harvest Room for lunch. After they ordered cocktails Jack said, "Give me the details of your claim, Ted."

"Well, there is not much to it, Jack. The owners had an abnormal number of change orders and we decided to quote the impact on our remaining contract work with each change order, as well as the estimated time extension required. However, the owners' project manager rejected both the estimate for impact on our contract work and the requested time extension."

"What reason did he give you?"

"His reason was that neither the impact cost nor the time extension can be accurately estimated, and he would entertain a claim for both of them only after project completion."

"Did he put this in writing?"

"Yes."

"I see. So what's his hang-up with your claim?"

"He says the figures are inflated."

"Are they?"

"I don't think so, Jack. We kept accurate records of all change orders during construction, including the remaining contract work at each stage. Furthermore, we had an undisrupted period in the beginning of construction that confirmed our labor estimates."

"It's a straightforward claim, then. I still don't understand what the project manager's hang-up is. What's his name, incidentally?"

"His name is Fred Ferdorski. I've known him for many years. I think he's just being obstinate—trying to impress the owners with his endeavor to protect their interests."

"To whom does he report?"

"He reports to a vice president by the name of Theodore Watkins. His office is in Calgary, but he spends most of his time in Edmonton—until the plant is operating."

Jack said, "I think I'll take a look at your records first. Then I'll see Fred Ferdorski, and if he's difficult, I'll make an appointment to meet with Mr. Watkins. Do you keep all project records in Edmonton?"

"Yes. They are located on the jobsite, Jack."

"Okay, Ted. Meet me here for breakfast tomorrow morning and we'll head out to the jobsite afterwards."

Jack spent most of the next day going over the records. Ted helped with retrieving and refiling. Finally Jack said, "I'm satisfied that we have a solid claim, Ted. Make me an appointment with Fred Ferdorski for the morning and then let's head back to the MacDonald."

Ted joined Jack for dinner at The Harvest Room. They discussed the possible objections the owners could bring up to MDF's claim. Ted confessed he could not think of any. Jack asked him, "How low was our tender?"

"About one percent," said Ted.

"Hmm. We can rule that out. Did we run into any snags on site to which the owners could point the finger?"

"None, other than the owners' change orders."

"Did we have any late material deliveries?"

"No. Everything arrived on time."

"This is certainly a puzzler," said Jack. "Well, I'll find out more tomorrow, I suppose. Let's order."

They ordered the sea bass special and a bottle of Chenin Blanc. "How is everything else going in your division, Ted?" Jack wanted to know.

"Competition is tough out here, Jack, but we're doing okay—nothing to write home about, but okay."

"Good, Ted. However, be ready to get raked over the coals at the upcoming managers' meeting."

"I know. I'm not looking forward to it. I disagree with Harry about this sort of embarrassment, Jack."

"It's Harry's way of keeping his managers keen, Ted. Don't lose too much sleep over it."

Jack met with Fred Ferdorski next morning, and, as he had suspected, the fellow was totally unreasonable. He only made a few unsupported statements and Jack bade him goodbye. Then he made an appointment to meet with Theodore Watkins in his site office.

Jack introduced himself and Mr. Watkins said, "What can I do for you, Mr. Malone."

"First, let me ask you if you're satisfied with MDF's performance."

"Nothing to complain about, as far as that is concerned, Mr. Malone."

"You are aware that MDF has a claim against you for impacts caused due to an abnormal number of change orders?"

"Yes, but our project manager has rejected the claim as being unreasonable."

"I know. I have just had a meeting with him, but I can assure you, Mr. Watkins, that I have gone over the figures with a fine-toothed comb and I am satisfied that the claim is in no way inflated."

"Well, I have your word against that of my project manager."

"Your project manager had our estimates for impact on our contract work with every quote we submitted for your change orders, Mr. Watkins, and he instructed us to resubmit these claims at the completion of the project, which we did. Our original estimates are not too far from the final claim amount."

Mr. Watkins looked somewhat surprised, as if he'd just heard something for the first time. "Can you leave that with me, Mr. Malone, and I'll get back to you?"

"Certainly, Mr. Watkins. You can reach me at the Fairmont Hotel MacDonald until tomorrow afternoon."

"I'll give you a call in the morning."

He did, and said, "Please resubmit your claim to my attention, Mr. Malone, and I'll have it processed."

"Thanks, Mr. Watkins."

22

Jack gave Harry a report regarding his meeting with Theodore Watkins the next day and Harry said, "I'm glad we weren't forced to take legal action on this claim Jack. Legal action is always a nasty business, even when you think you have a solid case. Can you meet me for lunch today, Jack? I have a few things I'd like to discuss with you and I'm a little short on time at present."

"The yacht club?"

"Yes."

After Harry ordered their cocktails he said, "Fiona is in the process of arranging our management meetings. We're meeting in Boca Raton this year and I would like you to prepare a presentation on the pros and cons of construction claims, Jack. You've gained a little more experience since our last management meeting, which should help with examples."

"Are you sure you want me to use our examples, Harry? They might be embarrassing."

"Use your best judgment, Jack. You don't have to mention any names. The dos and don'ts are sufficient."

"Why don't I draft a presentation and let you have a look at it?"

"No need to. I trust your discretion, Jack."

"Okay. I'll do my best."

"Before we leave for Boca Raton there's another matter I'd like you to look into. Henry Jackson has a disagreement with the City of Regina and he needs your help to resolve it." Harry was talking about MDF's Saskatchewan Division Manager.

"What seems to be the problem?"

"He's finished a contract with the City of Regina to install some underground piping. They ran into some buried foundations, which caused delays, and further delays happened because of heavy snowstorms. The city expressed its willingness to pay for the foundation delays but is unwilling to pay for bad-weather delays."

"In other words, they are taking a typical owners' position?"

"I believe there is more to it, Jack. Fly out there and meet with them. Try to get it resolved before we leave for Boca Raton."

"Okay."

"By the way, Fiona will ask Mary to come along to Boca Raton to assist her with the arrangements."

"I think Mary will like that."

"And how about you, Jack?"

When Jack arrived home he told Mary that he has planned to take her to an opera. Mary was surprised.

"I'm not too keen on operas, Jack," she said.

"You may like this one. It's one of my favorite operas."

"What's the name of it?"

"It's Puccini's *Madame Butterfly*."

"Oh, I've heard of it. It's about a Japanese geisha girl who had married a US sailor. They had one son, then he went back to America where he married an American woman. Then he returned to Japan with his American wife and his American wife wanted to adopt the son. However, the geisha wife was so distressed that she committed suicide.

"Oh, Jack, I'm not sure I'm up to watching such a sad opera just now."

"Okay, I'll take you to your favorite restaurant instead."

"I like that better."

While they enjoyed their dinner Jack told her about Boca Raton, and that Fiona planned to ask her to come along and help her with the arrangements.

Mary was all excited. "Will we visit your mother, too, Jack?"

"Of course, Mary. I wouldn't miss introducing her to my one and only life's partner, would I?"

"I'm certainly looking forward to meeting your mother, Jack."

Henry Jackson picked Jack up at the Regina airport. They stopped at a restaurant for lunch and Henry filled Jack in on more details of his claim. He also showed Jack the owners' general conditions of the specifications. Jack glanced through them and said, "I can see what the City bases its rejection of the claim on, Henry. The general conditions specifically allow for delay payments regarding the buried foundations, but they disallow delay payments for adverse weather conditions."

"But my counter argument to them is that the bad weather occurred during the extension period and not during the originally scheduled construction period."

"It's a good argument. Well, let's go and meet with them and find out if we can convince them."

They kept a two o'clock appointment with the City's construction manager, Willard Smith, and Henry introduced Jack.

"How can I help you, Mr. Malone?"

"It's regarding MDF's Claim, Mr. Smith. I realize that the general conditions exclude paying for delays caused by adverse weather, but I wonder if in this case you could make an exception because the bad weather occurred during the extended construction period as a result of the buried foundations' delay? I know that Henry has already given you this argument."

"Yes, but, unfortunately, our hands are tied, Mr. Malone. The City's legal department would never sanction an exception. The general conditions disallow delay payments for any contracted construction work, no matter when it occurs. I know that in this case the contracted construction work occurred during an extension caused by buried foundations, and the City agrees to pay for that delay. However, we cannot pay for the additional delay caused by the snowstorm. I hope you can understand our position on that."

"I can, but I was hoping to change your mind, Mr. Smith."

"Sorry. I think you are out of luck, Mr. Malone."

They shook hands, and Henry drove Jack back to the airport. "You can't win them all, Henry," said Jack.

23

Jack reported to Harry the next morning that their case in Regina was probably unwinnable. Harry shrugged his shoulders. "You can't win them all, Jack."

In the following days before leaving for Boca Raton Jack prepared a few comments on construction claims for the management meeting. He was tweaking his notes one evening when the phone rang. A man introduced himself and said he was calling to get a reference on Brian Forbes.

"Brian is a good construction division manager," Jack assured him.

"Why did he leave MDF?"

"It was a personal matter," said Jack.

"Okay, I won't delve into that. Would MDF rehire him?"

"It would certainly be my recommendation."

"Well, Thanks, Mr. Malone. I appreciate your comments."

"I'll be darned," Jack told Mary. "Brian took me up on my offer to supply him with a reference. That was a prospective employer on the phone."

Mary smiled knowingly, as if she had anticipated Brian's eventual response to Jack's offer.

After Jack returned to tweaking his notes, Mary said, "I wonder how your mother will receive me, Jack?"

"My mother will love you, Mary. She is a very understanding woman."

"You mean she will understand our common-law relationship?"

"I guess that's what I meant. I frankly hadn't even thought about it, with my preparations for the meeting. However, my mother will also understand that love is everything, regardless of the marital status."

"It's just that the previous generation was all for traditional marriage ceremonies, Jack. That will worry me when meeting your mother."

He put away his notes, got up, kissed her gently, and said, "You worry too much, Mary. My mother may be from the previous generation, but she is also a compassionate woman of the world."

Jack and Mary left early on Saturday morning for Boca Raton. They checked into separate but adjoining rooms at the Boca Beach Club. Fiona asked Mary to join her mapping out the next week's shopping trip for the ladies, so Jack decided to visit his mother.

Jack's mother lived in a bungalow near a park and had a maid come by three times a week to assist her with the household chores. The maid had weekends off and his mother made him an omelet for lunch. She had greeted him warmly and asked him why he hadn't brought his girlfriend.

"She's busy today helping Fiona," Jack told her.

"And I was looking forward to meeting her" his mother complained.

"You'll get to meet her next weekend, Mother, after our meetings are over. She has to assist Fiona during the next week."

"I see. Perhaps I could prepare us a dinner next weekend?"

"No need, Mother, I intended to invite you to join us for dinner at your favorite restaurant."

"Thanks, dear. Now tell me all about the love in your life."

"She is a wonderful woman—almost forty, brown hair and eyes, divorced, good-looking, and likes most of the things I like."

"Why did she get divorced?"

"Incompatibility—it happens."

"A person should know that before deciding to get married."

"Preferably, yes, but it does not always happen. Please don't embarrass her about it, Mother."

"Of course not—you know me better than that."

"As far as I am concerned, she's her ex's loss and my gain. I love her very much."

"I'm glad for you. For a while I was afraid you'd never get over the loss of Katherine." The reminder made him sad for a moment.

"I'm sorry. I guess I shouldn't have mentioned her."

"That's all right, Mother," Jack assured her. "I got over her soon after I met Mary."

"Do you intend to get married to her?"

"No need—our love for each other is all we want."

"I still have concerns about modern partnerships. In my days, we valued a proper Christian marriage."

"Mary and I are living happily together even without a 'proper Christian marriage,' Mother."

"If that's what you want, son, I won't raise an objection. Nevertheless, I shall welcome her as my daughter-in-law."

Jack gave her a hug and a kiss on the cheek. "Thanks, Mom. I love you, too."

That evening Jack told Mary about his mother's eagerness to meet her. Mary was visibly relieved. She kissed him passionately and they decided to turn in early and enjoy Jack's king-sized bed—and each other, of course.

On Sunday the men went golfing and the women enjoyed a massage and make-up session at the spa. In the evening they all got together for an official welcome reception. Harry had arrived with a companion he only introduced as Anita. Fiona told Jack that she was a professional Swedish model, whom Harry had met on one of his yacht excursions.

The hors d'oeuvres were fantastic. Fiona had surpassed herself this year. Besides oysters and prawns, there was lox from Labrador, smoked eel from Denmark, smoked sea bass from Chile, and cheeses like English Stilton, German Tilsiter, Danish Havarti, Dutch Gouda, and French brie, as well as the usual veggies, of course, like olives, cherry tomatoes, celery, carrots, pearl onions, and dill pickles. Fiona had also selected excellent French wines to go with the hors d'oeuvres.

Jack whispered to Mary that there would be a lot of loving tonight, with all the "aphrodisiacs."

Mary laughed. "I look forward to it."

Jack milled around and talked to MDF's various managers. However, he had the distinct feeling that their warm welcome from last year was subdued this year. He returned to Mary and said, "Anytime you're ready, we can leave."

"Let's go," she answered.

After they entered their adjoining hotel rooms Jack opened a bottle of Tokaji from the Hungarian wine region of Tokaj-Hegyalja, which he had picked up on Saturday. He poured two glasses of the wine, gave one to Mary, and they sat down in easy chairs.

"I lost my enthusiasm for the presentation Harry asked me to give, Mary."

"Why's that?"

"My popularity with our managers seems to have cooled considerably. I'm not sure any comments from me on construction delay claims will be welcome."

"Hmm. When did Fiona schedule you to give your presentation?"

"First thing in the morning."

"Why don't you ask Fiona to delay it for a couple of days? Tell her you need more time to prepare."

"How would that help?"

"It means, the managers would have to give their reports first, and have their performances criticized. After that, they might welcome your presentation."

"You have a point. I'll call Fiona right now and ask her to reschedule my presentation."

The Monday-to-Friday management meetings were scheduled to start at nine o'clock and finish at noon each day. Lunches and afternoons were free. The managers and their companions could golf, play tennis, suntan on the beach, or go sightseeing.

Monday's meeting treated current economic influences on construction. Each manager reported on conditions in his area and got suggestions for coping with them from the other managers. The atmosphere of the meeting was friendly.

During the next two meeting days each manager had to report on his division's performance over the last fiscal year and present his proposed budget for the next fiscal year. The performances in the Western Canada divisions were the worst and attracted much criticism from the Eastern Canada division managers. Tempers were flying high and Harry had to calm some managers down.

Fiona had rescheduled Jack's presentation for Thursday's meeting. He started with a statement about the estimate.

"The estimate should include foreseeable delays in construction."

"You've got to be kidding," said Mario Stefanos, the Hamilton Division Manager.

"Hold on," said Jack, "I haven't finished yet. What I mean is, each foreseeable delay also has a probability of its occurrence. If the probability is low, so is the value of its inclusion in the estimate. To disregard the possible event just because its probability of occurrence is low is irresponsible estimating."

"How many projects are you going to land that way, Jack?" asked Jim Rowe.

"You'll land fewer projects than you would when disregarding probable delays, I suspect, Jim. However, your estimated profit is more secure, and you're less likely being challenged by the owners for wanting to recover your estimating losses."

Harry nodded his agreement and Jack received no more objections on this point. He then presented a few examples of claims that could have been avoided and claims that were irresponsibly prepared. On the latter he received some objections, but Harry jumped in and explained to them that MDF's image must at all times be considered. Harry said he was not interested in profits at the expense of MDF's image.

"And let me add this," he said. "Jack has been instructed by me to guard MDF's image, so don't blame him for being critical of your claims."

Jack was glad about Harry's clarification. He noticed that most managers displayed a friendlier attitude towards him after this meeting. When he discussed the outcome of the meeting with Mary that evening, Mary said, "The timing of your presentation probably helped as well, Jack."

"Of course. And I have you to thank for your suggestion, Mary."

The last meeting day was Harry's day. He praised good performances and also leveled criticism where appropriate. Few managers were offended by his criticism, and the meeting ended with handshakes and good wishes—even congratulations for outstanding performances.

Friday evening was MDF's award night. After a sumptuous dinner Harry handed out bronze plaques to all managers who had exceeded their budgeted profit projections and the audience applauded each manager. Some managers who came close to their budgeted profit received an honorable mention from Harry and were also applauded.

For the remainder of the evening Fiona arranged to have an excellent dance band provide the entertainment and Jack and Mary enjoyed a few tangos together. During one dance break Mary asked, "Have you given any more thought as to which of the islands we should visit, Jack?"

"There are a couple of obvious ones: Paradise Island, near Nassau, and the Bermuda Islands."

"From what I hear, Paradise Island is popular if you like casinos. The Bermuda Islands are very colorful but hardly the most romantic, Jack."

"That's true," he said.

"How about we visit the Hawaiian Islands?"

He laughed. "Okay, sweetheart—the Hawaiian Islands it is."

Harry signaled Jack to join him at his table. Jack went over and sat beside Harry. Anita gave him a disinterested glance.

Harry asked, "When are you planning to return to Toronto, Jack?"

Jack suspected that when Mary had asked Fiona for an extra two-week vacation Fiona must have told Harry. "In about two weeks," he said.

"Where are you going from here?"

"Hawaii."

"Ah, that will be romantic. Can I ask you to make a stopover in Denver? I'm contemplating acquiring shares in Rocky Mountain Infrastructure Builders Inc. located in Denver, and I would like you to meet with the seller, George Sanders, and assess the share value for me, Jack. I can make an appointment with him for you—say for next Tuesday?"

"Okay," said Jack, getting up. "Nice meeting you, Anita." She gave him another disinterested glance.

As Jack rejoined Mary she said, "He has another assignment for you, I bet."

"He does, but he's not suggesting to cancel our Hawaii trip, Mary."

24

On Saturday, Jack and Mary drove to Orlando to visit Walt Disney World's Epcot theme park at Bay Lake, dedicated to human achievement. It was the first visit for both and they were awed by the displays. In the evening they drove back to Boca Raton.

After a leisurely walk on Sunday morning and a light lunch at the Boca Beach Club they drove to Jack's mother's bungalow. When his mother opened the door Jack introduced Mary to her. She greeted them warmly with a hug and led them into her living room.

Mary was obviously still a little shy. She said, "You have a lovely bungalow, Mrs. Malone."

"Call me Angie, Mary," Jack's mother insisted. "Yes, it's lovely, and I like the quiet neighborhood and the park nearby. The weather is bearable, too, in Florida."

Angie showed them around the house first, and then the garden at the back. It was a small garden, nicely laid out with flowers. "Planting vegetables would be like carrying coal to Newberry," she laughed.

"It's so peaceful here," Mary marveled. "I could enjoy this forever."

"Beautiful and peaceful," Angie added.

They spent the afternoon talking about everyday experiences and Mary explained to Angie that her parents also owned a lovely house in Winnipeg with a garden full of flowers.

"I'd like to meet your parents sometime," said Angie. "I'm not sure, though, it would be in Winnipeg. It's too cold for me there."

At six o'clock Jack drove them for dinner at Angie's favorite restaurant, the Casa D'Angelo. Angie ordered the gnocchi "Mamma," Mary ordered fettuccini Bolognese, and Jack ordered the lamb ragout with pappardelle and a bottle of vintage Chianti wine.

During dinner Angie asked if their planned trip to Hawaii is a honeymoon trip.

Jack laughed. "You could call it that, I suppose."

After dropping Angie off Mary said, "I like your mother, Jack. She is very sophisticated."

In the morning, after giving Jack's king-sized bed one more workout, they had breakfast and drove back to Orlando to board a flight to Denver. In Denver, they checked into the Four Seasons Hotel.

25

Jack called Rocky Mountain Infrastructure Builders the following morning to confirm his appointment with George Sanders, which had been arranged by Harry for ten o'clock.

When Jack arrived at RMIB George Sanders met him personally and took him into his large office. The office was sparsely furnished, but had quite a few pictures of infrastructure projects on the walls. Sanders noticed Jack looking at them and said, "These are only a few of the infrastructure projects we have built, Mr. Malone."

"Impressive," said Jack.

George Sanders had a tall, lean, six-foot-two-inch frame and was clean-shaven, with sharp facial features, keen eyes, styled white hair, and manicured fingernails. He wore a grey suit and mauve shirt with a designer-style silk tie. He was in his early seventies, Jack guessed, and his outer appearance was almost elegant.

After they sat down in easy chairs around a corner table and George Sanders poured their coffees Jack said, "Harry Broughton asked me to assess the value of your shares, Mr. Sanders."

"I know—Mr. Broughton told me that."

"Who else owns shares in your company?"

"My son and three junior partners, who also manage operational construction phases."

"Can I ask you why you don't sell your shares to them, Mr. Sanders, or keep them for your retirement?"

"Certainly. My junior partners have pretty well exhausted their financial resources, Mr. Malone, and my son also wants to sell his shares to build a plastic surgery clinic. He's not interested in the construction business. Besides, I have other investments in mind during my retirement. This company has reached a stage where it could use new blood—new ideas, as it were—to expand beyond the North American market."

"I see. How did you settle on Harry Broughton to sell your shares to, if I may ask, Mr. Sanders?"

"I might as well disclose that there are two more potential buyers, Mr. Malone. However, there won't be any negotiations regarding the selling price, nor will there be any bid peddling. My decision to whom to sell my shares will be strictly based on the qualifications of the prospective buyer. Right now I'm favoring Harry Broughton, simply because of his success with MDF. You can tell him that."

"I will," said Jack. Jack looked at him with some admiration. He knew he was looking at one of the giants in the construction industry—it was a rare privilege for him, indeed.

"What type of infrastructure projects does RMIB build, Mr. Sanders, and where do you mainly build them?" Jack enquired.

"We build all types of infrastructure—road and highway networks, including bridges, tunnels, etcetera; railways and terminal facilities, including signaling and communication systems; canals and navigable waterways; seaports and light houses; electrical generation plants and transmission lines; natural gas and petroleum pipelines, including pumping stations; water and sewage treatment plants; telephone and mobile phone networks; solid waste management; and so on. I could mention more, but this will give you the idea. Some of our building projects are displayed here on the walls, Mr. Malone. Furthermore, we are also involved with infrastructure management. As far as our area of operation is concerned, we presently limit ourselves to North America—including Canada, by the way—but we are looking to build in South America next."

"I must admit, I'm impressed. I had no idea about the wide-ranging scope of your company, Mr. Sanders. When can I have a look at your financial statements?"

"After you sign a confidentiality agreement I'll give you the last five years of our financial statements. I would prefer you looking at them in this office. You can use our boardroom, Mr. Malone."

"Fine. I'll come back after lunch."

Jack headed back to the Four Seasons and had his lunch with Mary. He told her about his meeting with George Sanders and how impressed he was with the operation of Rocky Mountain Infrastructure Builders.

Jack returned to RMIB's offices at two o'clock, signed the confidentiality agreement, and busied himself in the boardroom with the financial statements. What he discovered amazed him. RMIB's book value per share exceeded the asking price, probably because of the high investment in construction tools and equipment; the depreciated assets were well below market value; there was a steady increase in sales volume and profit over the last five years; and the company had no long-term debt. Jack had assessed a few companies in his career, but none came close to this company. Harry could consider himself lucky in case George Sanders decided to sell him his shares.

Late afternoon Jack met with George Sanders again and enquired, "Would I qualify to buy some shares in your company, Mr. Sanders?"

"That depends on whether you could meet my conditions, not only financially, but also as a manager of infrastructure construction phases. If you were able to meet these conditions, I suppose you could purchase my son's shares. He owns ten percent of RMIB. I would include my son's share with the sale of my shares, but I don't want any shareholder to own more than fifty percent of the company's shares."

"Let me discuss it with my partner and I'll get back to you, Mr. Sanders."

"Partner?"

"Sorry, my common-law spouse."

"I see. Certainly, discuss it with your partner, Mr. Malone. I gather, then, that you have the financial ability to purchase my son's shares and you can impress me with your construction management experience?"

"Yes to both, I believe."

"Good. Please send me your curriculum vitae as soon as possible."

Jack bade George Sanders goodbye and told him he would report to Harry Broughton and get back to him in the morning with his decision and his curriculum vitae.

After they finished their sumptuous dinner Jack told Mary about his opportunity to buy into RMIB and also work for them as a construction manager.

"That's wonderful, Jack," said Mary. "It will certainly solve your emotional problem having to expose the shortcomings of your friends."

"Yes, and it will also provide me with a new and challenging work horizon. But it may mean moving to Denver and postponing our Hawaii trip, Mary."

"I don't mind, Jack. I like Denver, and I'm sure there will be other opportunities for vacations."

He looked at her admiringly and smiled. What a partner!

The next morning Jack phoned Fiona and requested an appointment to see Harry. She asked him why he couldn't just email his report to Harry rather than disrupt their vacation. He explained to her that he wanted a face-to-face meeting with Harry, for personal reasons. Then he went to RMIB's offices to deliver his share-purchase decision and his curriculum vitae to George Sanders. George Sanders briefly studied the curriculum vitae, nodded, and promised to get back to Jack within a few days regarding the final purchase arrangements of his son's shares. After lunch, Jack and Mary boarded their flight to Toronto.

26

When they met Jack gave Harry a detailed assessment of the Rocky Mountain Infrastructure Builders' shares. He ended his report by saying, "Consider yourself lucky, Harry, if George Sanders decides to sell you his shares." Then he added, "I'm buying some shares myself, Harry."

Harry gave him a questioning look.

"These are additional shares available from George Sanders' son. He's a doctor and wants to use the money from the sale of his shares to open a plastic surgery clinic."

"I see," said Harry. "I could also buy the additional shares, though."

"George Sanders does not want one shareholder to own more than fifty percent of the shares."

"But if you buy the doctor's shares, together we would own more than fifty percent in any case."

"That is why I wanted to meet with you personally, Harry. George Sanders offered me a management position along with his son's shares."

"I see. Have you accepted the offer, Jack?"

"I have. It's not a matter of money, Harry. I'm unhappy with the investigator's job at MDF. I don't like to see people get fired because of my work here."

"I knew it would come to this eventually, Jack. When I offered you the position I had thought we had settled this issue, until I heard from Fiona that you were unhappy about the arrangement."

So much for trusting Fiona with anything, thought Jack.

Harry gave him a long look. Then, he said, "You're just kidding yourself, Jack, if you believe that you can change your vocation to get away from your emotional problems. Every top manager knows he cannot have emotional entanglements to do his job. The same applies to other professions—doctors, lawyers, policemen, and so on. None of them will reach the top of his or her profession with emotional entanglements."

Jack knew instinctively that Harry was right. He just thought that a management position would make things easier to handle as far as he was concerned. But he recalled an incident many years back when he should have fired an incompetent employee, but he kept him on—to his own detriment and to the detriment of the company—because he liked the guy. Finally Jack said, "Brian Forbes was a good manager, Harry. Yes, he made a mistake, but firing him for it was unfair, I think."

"I'm a firm believer in the Darwinian principle that desirable traits will systematically develop the best of the best, Jack. I don't fire employees because it gives me a kick. I fire them because I want to employ the best. I know people make mistakes—that may not be a good reason to fire them. In Brian's case, I did not fire him because he made a mistake. I fired him because he was dishonest. Dishonesty in business, as in many other professions, can have serious consequences, Jack. Dishonesty is not a mistake. It is an inherent trait that should be eliminated."

Harry gave Jack another long look. "You are tops in your job on the technical end, Jack, but you must learn to control your emotional side. You cannot use your emotions to excuse dishonesty—not as an investigator, not as a manager, and not in any other profession you may choose."

"I like to remind you, Harry, of my solution to bring our Instrumentation Division back into the black. As I told you at the time, Frank Butler, the Consortium owners' engineer, unreasonably cut back Joe Kaluzniak's estimates for extra work, which resulted in a heavy loss on the contract. When I was in Edmonton Joe Kaluzniak was just pricing another large extra to the contract—the last one before job completion. I saw an opportunity to make back some of Frank Butler's unfair cutbacks and told Joe to triple the labor for the extra. I knew that Frank Butler could not hire another contractor to do the work, and time was of the essence. In other words, we had him over a barrel, for a change. He had to approve our estimate to finish the project on time. My solution was certainly dishonest, Harry, and you knew it. Why didn't you fire me?"

Harry looked at Jack with contemplation.

"You accuse me of being too emotional," Jack continued. "Perhaps you're right, but I want to be quite frank with you, Harry. It's just the hypocrisy that gets me. You want to have your cake and eat it too. You want the profits your managers produce for you, and you want the world to view you as an honest man. I do not believe there are many successful businesses that reached their level of success by being entirely honest. The truth is you don't want your dishonesty exposed. It's all right as long as you can get away with it and be viewed as an honest man. Your kind of honesty, Harry, is nothing more than a travesty, an inferior imitation."

While Jack was talking Harry developed an expression of dismay. Both men were silent for a long time. Harry's expression gradually changed to sadness, as if he had come to some unexpected realization for the first time. Finally he said, "I wish you luck in your new job with RMIB, Jack."

"Thanks, Harry. I think I'll need it. RMIB's type of construction will be a new challenge for me."

Both men got up, shook hands, and went their separate ways.

About the Author

Arthur Thormann realized he wanted to be a writer as a teenager after composing his first poem, which he wrote for his mother. He has spent most of his working life in management roles within the industrial construction sector. His experiences dealing with construction delay claims provide first-hand fodder for *Honesty's Travesty* protagonist, Jack Malone. He still writes poetry, acts as a consultant to contractors, and develops software as a hobby. Of German birth, Thormann lives in retirement with his wife and eldest daughter and writes prolifically — to date he has published over a dozen books. His chosen home is in Edmonton, Alberta, along the beautiful Saskatchewan River valley.

www.ingramcontent.com/pod-product-compliance
Lightning Source LLC
Chambersburg PA
CBHW060032210326
41520CB00009B/1100